To Dear Bernie
With our love and gratitude
for your prayers. Rosemary & Eric

HELPING HIS
HUNGARIAN HEROES

BY

GW00707748

ERIC C. BARRETT

Published by
'4H'
Helping HIS Hungarian Heroes
Backwell, North Somerset BS48 3JZ

© 2003 *'4H'*
First English Edition 2003

All rights reserved.
No part of this publication may be reproduced or transmitted
in any form or by any means, electronic or mechanical,
including photocopy, recording or any information or
storage and retrieval system, without permission
in writing from the publisher.

ISBN 9545160 0 1

All Scripture quotations in this book, except those noted
otherwise, are from the New International Version,
Copyright © 1973, 1978, 1984 by
New York International Bible Society,
and are used by permission.

Design and word-processing by
Eric and Rosemary Barrett
Cover design by Marco Cazzulini
Maps by Drew Ellis

Printed in Great Britain for
'4H'
44 Hilldale Road, Backwell, North Somerset, BS48 3JZ by
J W Arrowsmith Ltd. of Bristol, BS3 2NT

DEDICATION

To
two wonderful ladies:
Gillian in the past,
and Rosemary in the present.
- both precious gifts from God -
for all their love,
help and support.

CONTENTS

Foreword

Preface

1:      Scene-setting Sketches   13

2:      The Where, When and What
of the Hungarian World   27

3:      Toothbrushes, Teddy Bears
and Many Other Things   45

4:      Building for Eternity   59

5:      The Flipchart Flurry   89

6:      Higher Hurdles   107

7:      Hidden Treasure   129

8:      The Circle Widens   143

9:      Two-way Traffic   163

10:      Our Highest Calling   175

Other Selected Books   189

Answers to Chapter 2 Quiz   190

'4H' - A Summary   191

FOREWORD

I met Dr. Eric Barrett and his first wife Gillian as Pastor of the Győr Baptist Church and its district a number of years ago. A British group was working on the renovation and painting of the new church building in Papa, and Eric was their leader. We understood each other very quickly, and the presence and ministry of those visitors proved to be a blessing for all of us.

The following years I had the possibility to meet many times with the Barretts and with the 'Practical Teams' led by them. It was so nice to feel that they seriously paid attention to our needs, and they helped in constructive and encouraging ways.

Then it was a great experience when - in the course of our broadening ministry - my wife Csilla and I visited several churches in England and Wales. The Barretts were wonderful helpers in organising our trip.

Indeed, since those earlier times in the middle to late 1990s, our lives, our spiritual and ministerial growth have grown together at many points. We ourselves have been gladdened to see how their own ministries have widened in Hungary: Pápa, Kőszeg, Győr, Sárvár, Komárom, Bicske, Orgovány, Recsk and other places… with Nyírbátor planned to be the next.

Of course, not only the reconstructing groups have been important, but all the evangelising activities and presents too, all the inputs and tools that can be used for God's glory in new or older congregations and by church planters.

The ministry of Dr. Eric Barrett - I believe - has contributed to the spiritual awakening of the western Hungarian region in particular, and to the founding of new churches and their growth.

Thanks go to all those churches and persons in the United Kingdom who have supported these efforts. We remember with thankfulness the groups, the preachers, the children's workers, all the ministers… and all those who stay at home, but give and pray to make these ministries possible. We are grateful to all these dear friends for their love towards Hungary.

My congratulations to Eric and his new wife, Rosemary on the writing and publishing of this book, which raises the attention to the love of God Himself, that spans all international borders. I trust and expect that this fascinating account of the way He leads, guides and empowers His children will be a great blessing to every one who reads it.

Soli Deo Gloria!... the glory is God's alone!

Lelkipásztor Papp János
Mission Secretary
Hungarian Baptist Union
Budapest   June 2003

PREFACE

On Sunday, March 2003 I enjoyed sharing the Word of God with a little country chapel congregation in Egerszolát in north-eastern Hungary. Meanwhile, members of the congregation of my own church in Bristol, England were receiving its weekly digest of notices in the *Newslink*, plus an additional *'Special News Bulletin'*.

One side of my plain but decidedly dramatic sheet of paper described: *"A new 'mission'"*. It explained how, after nearly 36 years of happy, fulfilling and varied service with the Slavic Gospel Association literally all over the world I had become sure that, along with a fine group of Trustees, I should establish a new and complementary Charitable Trust focussed more specifically on the Hungarian speaking region of eastern and central Europe.

By way of answering the question: *"Why would anyone ever sever links with a Christian organisation after such a long period of rewarding work if retirement was not on the agenda,"* I wrote: *"With difficulty!"*

But I was already able to explain that it was: *"Because I feel overwhelmingly led of the Lord to do so - and in the six weeks or so since the final decision was made, I have been astonished by all the encouragements I have received in this and related areas of my life."*

The chief purpose of this new book is to describe more of the needs and opportunities to help Hungarian Christians as they seek to live for the Lord and spread news of His love for all in their homelands. The Hungarians are still relatively neglected in the thinking, planning and actions of Christian communities elsewhere: hence the great scope for us to encourage them through *'4H'*. However, another major purpose of this volume is to honour God through accounts of some of the many things that have recently been accomplished in the Hungarian region with His aid and in His name. Yet another is to honour the many from the UK who have already helped us help Hungarians. Last but by no means least I hope this account will stimulate others to want to do so too.

Meanwhile, what of the other side of that: *'Special News Bulletin'*? This was headed: *"And a new marriage!"* In early 1967 I was newly engaged to Gillian, and it was together that we were asked to serve engaged to Gillian, and it was together that we were asked to serve the Lord through SGA from that time. She was to be a truly wonderful wife and fellow worker for the Lord until she was called into the visible presence of her Saviour on 30 September 2002. Chapter 10 will then relate how in the remarkable providence of God, and on the very day of the inaugural Trustees Meeting of *'4H'*, I first heard of Rosemary and she heard of me. Five days later Rosemary and I met, and immediately both sensed He had much planned for us together. What an answer to the prayers of many on my behalf, and to my own question: "I know You wish me to continue in a mission capacity - but HOW?"

So I am even more strongly reminded as I write this Preface than I was when I wrote this volume as a whole that God says: *"For My thoughts are not your thoughts, neither are your ways My ways"* (Isaiah 55:8). As I further remarked in that Special Bulletin, *"His love, imagination and power are truly on leagues of their own!"*

In concluding this brief opening statement, it is my pleasant duty to thank the many who have helped bring this account into being. In particular I must thank by name David Clarke from Claverham who has so often and selflessly answered my frantic SOS messages when I have been unable to control my personal computer - a device I had not even switched on until after Gillian's illness was first diagnosed in February 2002. Shirley Sparks, my former secretary from the University of Bristol, plus her sons Jonathon and Peter, have also given much-needed computing help at crucial times. I am also much indebted to the Trustees of *'4H'* for their wisdom and encouragement, and to all of you who have prayed and given of yourselves in other ways to prosper this new venture.

What a joy it is, too, to acknowledge my new wife Rosemary, most especially for the loving and gracious way in which she has come into my life and is so glad to respond to the Lord's call to share this ministry. And of course it is a continuing pleasure, blessing and delight to be able to serve Him among and alongside our Hungarian Brothers and Sisters in Christ. On behalf of all of us in *'4H'* I extend our very warmest Christian love and gratitude to them.

Dr. Eric C. Barrett
Backwell, North Somerset   April 2003

MAP 1: Hungary today (stippled), and before the 1920 Treaty of Trianon (cross hatched).

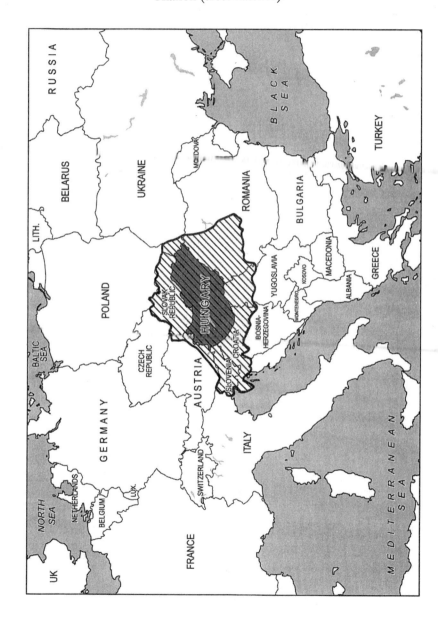

MAP 2: Hungary today, showing places mentioned in the text.

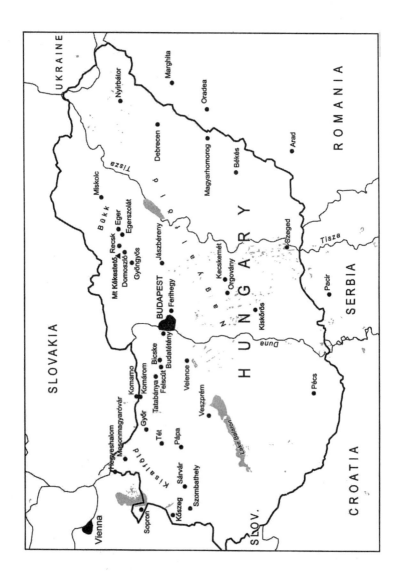

CHAPTER 1

SCENE-SETTING SKETCHES

It was a nasty night at the very end of winter. There in the middle of Hungary's *Nagyalföld*, or 'Great Plain', the first big, bright, fluffy flakes of snow were swirling over the silvered landscape from clouds which were about to wipe away the large and luminous moon. There were no house lights anywhere to be seen as we carefully negotiated the narrow, unfenced lanes across that flat area which owes much to the mighty Danube river even though that was still many miles away.

Coming to the dim outskirts of the little country town of Kiskőrös I marvelled that our driver could find his way, for there were no street lamps, and no names on many of the unmetalled side-roads so far as I could see. Suddenly, though, we approached a long, low building which showed a few lit light-bulbs in its courtyard: somehow we had arrived at the Charismatic church which was our destination. Several cars were strewn haphazardly on the grass verges nearby. Even more promisingly, clusters of young people were converging on the simple structure seemingly from all directions.

Parking up and joining the throng we found the courtyard literally buzzing with activity... and the interior of the simple church already packed. Once I had managed to de-steam my spectacles and we had found some seats, tight-wedged together, I scanned the congregation and guessed it to be an astonishing three hundred strong. What was even more amazing was that almost everyone apart from us must have been in their teens or twenties. True, the meeting was part of a youth conference, but I vainly tried to recall when I had last witnessed such a crowd of young people assembled for a Christian meeting in a small town in the United Kingdom.

Thereafter the whole event was to prove an exhilarating, uplifting and completely unforgettable experience. Young friends in colourful, casual 'international' clothes linked arms and swayed gently but rhythmically to the devotional songs, some unselfconsciously raising their hands aloft as they worshipped God, though all praised Him with intensity and enthusiasm. I was glad to be given a private, precise and quick-fire translation of the testimonies and Bible talks. This task was to be a veritable test of stamina for our young Hungarian companion Lilla, for the service lasted every minute of three hours, and maybe only one third of it was comprised of musical items which needed no interpretation. Despite the length of the proceedings, we saw nothing but rapt attention on the faces of the whole of that youthful audience, and I grew aware that I was the only person who had begun to fidget towards the end.

As I muse on that strongly-focussed congregation early in the Twenty-first Century I find my mind flitting back over the three-and-a-half decades since I first visited Hungary, beginning with some contrasts and comparisons between that memorable meeting in Kiskőrös and the first church service I had ever attended in the land of Hungary....

****

Thinking of comparisons, at least it may be said that, way back in 1965 Debrecen's *Nagytemplom* - the 'Big Church' - had also been crowded with worshippers. However, most of them were older women, though some elderly men were present too. Just a few younger people clustered together near the back of the austere, classically styled Lutheran sanctuary. There were no children anywhere to be seen. The ladies were mostly clad in thick, plain skirts and jumpers, their hair hidden beneath simply patterned kerchiefs. Many wore the black of perpetual mourning for, in the mid-1960s, such was still the uniform of widows and widowers across much of central, southern and eastern Europe. Most other men, despite Debrecen's role as a regional administrative centre of over 100,000 people, also had a rustic look for, in the Hungarian world 20 years of communism had done little to raise the living standards of even the urbanites. Almost all were still very poor, having to grow most of their food in their own back yards.

Neither old nor young ever had cash to spare on luxuries like 'designer' clothing - nor, indeed, anything other than the plainest, strongest and simplest dress. That very morning, with several new friends, I had ridden the tram into town from the university campus where we were all spending several weeks at an International Summer School. One of our group from England who - unusually - spoke quite good Hungarian already, told us afterwards that he had overheard an exchange between two other passengers, concerning of all things - his SHIRT! To us this was nothing special, but someone had wonderingly observed: "It's white, but has narrow pink and blue stripes!"

"Yes," enthused his younger companion, "and where they cross, there are small, purplish squares...!"

Back in the *Nagytemplom*, I myself was much more excited by the dignity and intensity of the uncomplicated service... the precisely-tuneful singing of these people who deserve the same reputation for musicality in their region as the Welsh enjoy in theirs... and the close attentiveness with which they listened to the preaching of God's Word. How reverently too they stood for prayer and the Bible readings! But what really startled me was something totally unexpected - the high values of the Forint bank notes in the overflowing offering plates as they were passed around. Clearly everyone present was glad to be able to worship God in that place, even though their government - in keeping with every other one at that time across half the continent, and beyond - frowned heavily on faith in Him. But most impressively of all, those impoverished people were, without doubt, committed not only to living, but also to giving, in truly sacrificial ways.

So, there was much to ponder as I returned to the university after that memorable morning service. In the Summer School, in addition to many east European students, there were groups of us from several western European countries. We were particularly closely watched by 'secret police' agents, though they themselves were so un-secret that we all knew exactly who they were. We all made sure that, when they were near, our conversations would be very bland. Such agents of the communist state were the chief reason why, after the *Nagytemplom* service, I had made no effort to speak with any of the congregation. It would have been great to have been able to at least exchange some greetings with a few of those fellow Believers... but I was well aware that this could have caused them sorry consequences. For, did not the *Hungary Today* book given each of us on the university course insist that:

"In Hungary everyone is aware that the (Communist) Party... which fights against all bourgeois views in order to strengthen Marxist-Leninist consciousness, is opposed to religious ideology, that tends to enslave the mind.... We all live, move about, and exist in this Marxist-Leninist reality.... He who sees this and adheres to the Marxist-Leninist creed has a present, and WILL HAVE A FUTURE...!"

No, the Hungarian government of that time did not begin to understand the deep truths of George Matheson's old hymn which affirms: *"Make me a captive Lord, and then I shall be FREE...".* Much worse, Christians under communism in Hungary came to suffer much for their faith, some even in prisons or prison camps. In the meantime, other Hungarian Christians outside Hungary itself, as we shall see later in this book, were threatened starkly, merely because they too were committed to live for the Lord.

****

Many years later my first wife Gillian and I heard of one specially sobering situation in which Hungarian Believers suffered intensely for the sake of Jesus Christ. It was the autumn of 2001. We were in the little village of Recsk, high in the Mátra Mountains over 100 miles north-east of Budapest, and literally in the shadow of the country's highest peak, Mount Kékestető.

Why were Gillian and I there with a dozen or so other friends from Bristol and nearby? As Chapter 4 will explain more fully, our purpose was to help renovate and redecorate a little Baptist chapel, and help make it more suitable for church activities 100 years after it was built, and 50 years after its previous very limited face-lift.

One afternoon, after a long day's work, Pastor Imre piloted a few of our Team up a rough and winding road to a huge quarry we had seen high on a hill above the village.

"Early in the communist era," Imre explained, "Recsk became a special byword for terror. In the 1950s, soon after the first communist government took control in Budapest, the regime cut out this concentration camp among the pinewoods, and forced the prisoners to work the rock."

There, more than 2000 feet above sea level in that harsh continental interior, the winter weather was even more extreme than in the valleys below. Temperatures often dropped to below -35 degrees Celsius, yet thickly clad guards always insisted that the work go on regardless.

Today just one replica dormitory hut, roughly constructed of split tree trunks, bears witness to the awful living conditions the many prisoners of conscience faced when finally each shift was done. When we visited, it was too late in the day to go inside, but gaps between the logs were wide enough for that not to matter: we could easily peer in. Every winter awful bone-chilling winds would have whistled in through such cracks, adding acute physical pain to the extreme discomforts of overcrowding, zero personal privacy, earthen floors, rough-hewn benches and bare sleeping platforms.

Work outside was enforced in literally all weathers - from the icy blasts of winter to the heat, high humidity and torrential thunderstorms of summer. Meanwhile, awaiting inmates who somehow further incurred the wrath of sadistic guards, there were tiny below-ground detention cells the shape and size of open graves. These were crudely roofed to keep the prisoners from getting out, but not to prevent rain, snow and hail from getting in. And there was cruel symbolism in that shape and size, for multitudes of men and women died in that dreadful camp. Many of the victims went unrecorded, nameless at least as far as local officialdom and the nation's government were concerned.

Today, near the entrance to the complex, there stands a modern monument of artfully arranged broken concrete blocks. These carry the names of some of those considered opponents of the state who are known to have perished in the camp, but it is beyond question that the list is very incomplete. It is well known, too, that many who died in the concentration camp at Recsk were committed followers of Jesus Christ. Like the first martyr, Stephen, they lived and died bravely, proving that nothing could separate them from the eternal love of their dear Lord.

****

We had earlier discovered that in the communist 'Old Days' - as they are now obliquely called in Hungary - action against Believers was not only applied physically within Hungary itself, but also psychologically in places seemingly far beyond the reach of the communist authorities. In 1980, Gillian and I were given a vivid glimpse of this, in the most unlikely setting of our own home in Bristol.

Visiting us at that time were a Hungarian, the Rev. Joseph Steiner and his American wife, Marge. We had first met them a decade or so earlier on one of our working visits to the studios of Trans World Radio, the celebrated Christian station based in Monte Carlo, Monaco. In that exotic location on the sun-drenched, south-facing coast of the French Mediterranean Riviera, Monte Carlo was, and in many ways still is, a fabled 'playground for millionaires'. However, it has long been also a haven for Christian missionaries, most drawn there by the powerful shortwave transmitters on Mount Agel, high above the posh little Principality. From our very first visit in 1968, TWR's businesslike offices and peaceful sound-proofed studios had always seemed at least a world away from the drab cities and depressed villages behind the Iron Curtain which were among the 'prime target' areas for the invisible yet powerful and easily-accessed waves of radio.

Quietly gracious, smiling, bespectacled and prematurely balding, Joseph Steiner was introduced to us as: "The Hungarian Department of TWR". Already he had been for several years the only Bible broadcaster to the 20 million or so souls who spoke that unique and fascinating tongue. Through that visit to Monte Carlo, and others in later years, we got to know Joseph and Marge very well. Indeed, Joe's fertile mind, and enthusiasm for new and fresh ways to share the good news of the Gospel soon became a significant stimulus to my own. One particular result of this was to be the *Radio Academy of Science* programme which I designed and developed for SGA, and for which I wrote scripts all the time it was on the air to the former USSR and other countries from 1980 to 1993. Written originally in English, the scripts were translated first into Russian, then into several other languages. So the episodes, or excerpts from them, came to be transmitted to many parts of the world, including Hungary itself as described in greater detail in Chapter 6.

Meanwhile, in 1980 Gillian and I were privileged to welcome Joe and Marge as guests in our Bristol home, having arranged for them to participate in a special missionary weekend in our large, downtown church. During that stay we learned of a visit they themselves had been paid in their home in Monte Carlo. Unheralded in advance, it involved two members of Hungary's secret police of that time, the dreaded *AVH*.

"We know much about your radio messages to Hungary," the unwelcome visitors had coldly declared to Joseph, "and we know we can do nothing directly to stop them. But our government wishes them to cease. Should you <u>insist</u> on continuing with your broadcasts, our bosses will see to it that YOUR RELATIVES WHO ARE STILL IN HUNGARY WILL PAY THE PRICE!"

When we heard this we were literally moved to tears. For a few moments I was unable to respond. At last I was able voice my tortured thoughts: "I have heard much, and even seen a little first hand of the cost of Christian service in communist countries" I ventured slowly. "But to me the thought that <u>someone else</u>, especially SOMEONE I LOVE, might suffer because of what I felt I had to do for the Lord seems to me the VERY HIGHEST PRICE anyone could be asked to pay for doing that!"

And I still think so today.

How would YOU feel in a similar situation?

And how would you respond?

"Well," you may ask, "before giving an answer, how did <u>Joe</u>?"

And I would reply: "By <u>continuing</u> with the work to which he KNEW God had called him! Joe was well aware that his was the most widely-heard single voice encouraging his Hungarian Christian compatriots to stay true to the Lord, come what may... but also the only one many unbelievers could hear that urged them to turn to God for personal forgiveness and spiritual healing. So how could he <u>possibly</u> stop?!"

Some twenty years or so later, in the post-communist era and in the course of a message to a Hungarian village church congregation on the cost of Christian service, I mentioned Joseph Steiner and his determination to serve God regardless of the price he or others might have to pay. To my surprise there were at first blank, unresponsive looks when I said his name.

Then, suddenly, the face of one elderly lady lit up, as if a switch had been flicked. "Ah, SHTAY-nair YO-zeff!" she exclaimed excitedly, reversing the first name and family name in the usual Hungarian fashion - and giving both for the first time in my hearing their correct Magyar pronunciations!

At once other faces around the little church lit up too as heads nodded vigorously, and smiles shone everywhere. OF COURSE they knew him! Why had I not called him by his <u>proper</u> name...?!

After the service, Gillian and I were mobbed by those dear senior saints, all eager to recount something of what Joe's radio messages had meant to them in the 'Old Days' when any of 'The Faith' had been so strongly frowned upon. The concentration camp at Recsk had been not far away, and 'YO-zeff's' ministry had been a special help and cheer to them as they had sought to go on walking with the Lord.

"We would never miss a single programme," they averred. "and everyone else would know just when the broadcasts were about to begin, because all the Believers in the fields or elsewhere would hurry home to listen. That's how many unbelievers came to know when to listen too, and some of them were saved!"

And 'YO-zeff' still broadcasts once a week today, early every Saturday afternoon. Thus his elderly friends further enthused: "We thank God SO MUCH for him! Do you know where he lives now? You do? Please send him our love, and THANK HIM for so faithfully sharing his knowledge of the Word of God with us all over so many years!"

Unexpectedly, such was to be our privilege not long afterwards. In September 2001 we were able to visit Joe and Marge in their modest, rent-free little home near the west coast of Florida in the USA. Bradenton Missionary Village was purpose-built in 1981 for such dedicated servants of God who have spent all their lives serving Him, giving no thoughts to their own bank balances or future needs. That homely haven wholly owes its existence to

Anthony T. Rossi, the Italian-born immigrant who became the founder of the world-renowned *Tropicana* fruit juice company. It is a sunny, spacious and relaxing estate where neighbours are not only friends and neighbours but also fellow Believers in the Lord.

Gillian and I cherished that six-hour opportunity to visit with Joe and Marge, and to be able to cheer and encourage them with the news that many friends, far away in Joe's beloved homeland, still listened regularly to his programmes, with true thanksgiving in their hearts.

I have also felt specially privileged to be able to get to know, and on several occasions work with, some of Joe's relatives in Hungary. They include some of those whose livelihoods - and persons - had been so directly threatened while Joe had been broadcasting from Monte Carlo in the bad 'Old Days'. I have learned from these heroic people that they themselves had been aware of such dangers through those dark decades. But they had been conscious too of the Lord's everlasting arms around them to keep them safe.

And He did indeed protect and preserve them through all that time, despite every threat - including those which had been made indirectly, so many miles away in millionaire-row Monaco....

****

My personal memories now move forward to late May 2002.

Once again the scene is the hill country village of Recsk, straggling along one of the valleys radiating from the high hub of Mount Kékestető down towards its rim. I was again visiting Pastor Imre and his family. The first reason was to present a set of 'Flipchart Books' for use in the Sunday Schools of the six upland fellowships which Imre and his wife Erika lead. Another reason was to give an outreach talk in the new village Community Centre, an attractive structure built recently in the village in a locally sympathetic style.

I was interested to know what advance publicity had been given to the talk, fully conscious that merely 12 years earlier even to give the talk itself would have been impossible. Nor could it have been given through the whole of any of the preceding half century, because of the strong aversion the communists had to the Christian faith.

"Did you announce the event in the local paper?" I innocently asked.

"There hasn't been one recently," came the unexpected reply from Imre's wife. She continued in even more surprising fashion: "It's only printed when there is enough news to make up an issue."

"So we used the 'town crier' instead," Imre chipped in.

And, perfectly on cue, sounds of a mobile loudspeaker swelled until, quite distinctly, I could hear it pronouncing something about an: " *'English professor', Dr Barrett Eric...* " !

Later that same day, the network of amplifiers on the mayor's office and other relatively prominent buildings, plus many telephone poles along the main street of the village, took up the theme and echoed it to all in earshot. That electronic-age town-crier system, originally an integral part of the communist effort to control not only the lives but also the minds of the people across virtually all of central and eastern Europe, was now serving as a loud, clear voice of the Gospel. How greatly things had changed since my first visit to Hungary in the mid-1960s!

I then remembered how, during a previous visit in September 2001, one of our Practical Mission Teams had worked so hard, along with the few able-bodied men from Imre and Erika's group of little churches, to renovate and redecorate their main chapel in Recsk. At the end of that week a reporter from *Recski Hírmondó*, that very-occasional newspaper, had come to see what the British people had been up to.... And I had spent well over an hour with the somewhat august lady. She had been described as: 'One of the most important people in the district'. A teacher in the nearby school, she had been a Communist Party bigwig before democracy had been restored to Hungary in 1990. She still enjoys publishing her views - even though their tone has had to change quite drastically. Indeed, once an atheist, this lady is now apparently interested in the occult.

Thus, my interview with her was one I had looked forward to with particular interest. It was a special opportunity to explain as clearly as I could that the Christian faith is not some empty, old-fashioned superstition, but a vital, up-to-date experience that every person needs.

The article about our Seventh Practical Mission subsequently appeared in the *Recski Hírmondó* in October 2002. We were glad to find that it proved to be both factual and reasonably sympathetic.

We continue to pray for this 'most important lady', that she will continue her personal exploration path all the way from communist dogma, through witchcraft, to the liberating truths of the Gospel of Jesus Christ. In keeping with so many of her compatriots, her mind is now open to His good news. Praise God that, after so many difficult and dangerous years, this can now be once again loudly and lawfully proclaimed across their land.

****

Great though it is today that the Christian message is no longer strongly opposed by the government in Hungary, it is even greater to see souls responding to it, especially when many of those coming to faith are in the broadly-defined 'young persons' category. For, as I remarked to interpreter friend Lilla at the end of that lively youth session described at the opening of this chapter: "If these young people are the future leaders and backbones of church fellowships of tomorrow, then the future of Christ's Kingdom in Hungary will be bright!"

However, I rejoiced all the more that several had responded to the final altar-call to commit themselves for the first time to His love and care. Truly the Holy Spirit had been present and active in that meeting, glad of the liberty there is now to transform lives with no fear of official retribution.

As we drove gingerly away from Kiskőrös through the by then thickly-falling snow I was grateful to God that such a tremendous transformation had come about in the fortunes of Hungarian churches since that first service I had witnessed in Debrecen's *Nagytemplom* in the mid-1960s. At that time so few young people had dared even to enter a place of worship. Now they can make public commitments to follow Christ, and join forward-looking fellowships like that in Kiskőrös, full to bursting with teens and twenties, without fear of being called to possible martyrdom. This contrast is all the stronger for it is just one expression of the continental-scale miracle which has swept across eastern Europe and beyond in recent years, permitting millions to enjoy freedom of faith where for so long the chance to believe was so slim and often very costly.

My own view of this miraculous metamorphosis squares perfectly with the personal reflections of a young Hungarian pastor's wife, Pálma. Her thoughts have been sweetly and succinctly expressed in the poem with which the recent book: *Glimpses of God's Grace*, which Gillian and I edited for SGA, concludes. Reprinted below, her verses tell how decades of totalitarian terror have given way to times of openness to worship the Lord and do His bidding relatively unafraid. Praise God that, despite local nuances and variations, the same type of transformation has swept across the whole Hungarian-speaking world - not just Hungary itself. This includes significant sections of some of its 'next door neighbour' countries too, as the next chapter proceeds to explain.

Pálma grew up in a devoted Christian home in Hungary, when to be a committed Christian was very perilous. More recently she has come to revel in the transformed situation as it is today. Her poem simply yet poignantly sums up the differences. It also stresses that zeal for the Lord, as outworked by people like her Dad, has not changed. It was intense, and remains so now. With absolute accuracy she describes folk like him as 'HEROES'. These are the ones we from the West have been, and still are privileged to serve as 'HELPERS', and whom the Lord is now leading us in *'4H'* to focus on with new and even greater vigour than before. Hence the title and the theme of this whole book, and the name and ethos of the newly established charity which others and I are now privileged to serve.

HEROES AND HELPERS

This little girl peeped as
  foreigners entered her home,
  their faces familiar,
  though their names were not known.

They were highly discreet -
  sensitive to the law -
  as they brought Bibles and love,
  a new coat, doll or more.

The helpers were taking a risk
  so they parked at a distance,
  sometimes tracked by police
  offering unwanted assistance.

After darkness had fallen
   they'd return to their car,
    then slip back with the goods
    prayed in from afar.

Yet the HERO to me
   was this little girl's Dad,
    keen for life-giving books
    our land did not have.

Father could lose his job,
   even end up in prison,
    but he loved God so much
    he continued His mission.

Today this girl's a mum
   in a new space and time,
    free to share hope with all
    and help Christ's life to shine.

Praise God, Bibles are welcome,
   His truths openly preached,
    and HIS HEROES, like Dad,
    STILL SEEK OUT THE UNREACHED!

CHAPTER 2

THE WHERE, WHEN AND WHAT OF THE HUNGARIAN WORLD

Everyone has heard of Hungary - but by setting friends a simple quiz I have found that many British people do not know very much about it. Maybe you would like to assess your own knowledge of the background to this book? If yes, try to answer the following twenty-point questions. The solutions are given on page 190. You must not peep until you have jotted down answers to each one! While being interesting, and a bit of fun, the quiz has its serious side too. It is widely recognised that the best prayers any of us can pray are <u>informed</u> prayers. To pray these we need some knowledge and understanding not only of the work God's heroes do in a particular region, and how best we may try to help them, but also of the context in which all of that work is set.

So, here are some basic questions about Hungary and certain of its neighbours:

1. Modern Hungary has borders with seven other nation states, Which are they? *(Name them for one point each).*
2. Today Hungary has about 5, 10, 20, 35 or 50 million people? *(Pick the correct number for one point).*

3. Hungary is largely comprised of the flood plains of which major European river and some of its tributaries? *(One point for the correct answer).*

4. What is the capital of Hungary? *(One point).*

5. What is Hungary's unit of currency called? *(One point).*

6. How long has Hungary been a recognised nation state: about 10, 50, 100, 500 or 1000 years? *(One point).*

7. Give two reasons why the 'Treaty of Trianon' in 1920 was - and still is - so disastrous for Hungarians. *(One point each).*

8. Why are (a) 1956; and (b) 1990 such significant dates in recent Hungarian history? *(One point each).*

9. Name the two historically dominant Christian denominations in Hungary. *(One point each).*

10. Is Hungary a member of (a) the Warsaw Pact; or (b) NATO? *(One point).*

11. Is Hungary a member of the European Union, yes or no? *(One point).*

Now check the answers on p.190.

How did you score out of a possible maximum of 20 points? Over 15 correct is very good; under 10 is - sadly! - what most British Christians get, so if you did so too, you are not alone. However, as a school report might put it: "There is much room for improvement!" But how ever many - or few - you scored, by the time you have read the whole of this book you will know more about it. So you will be much better placed to support God's work in Hungary and its neighbours, whether you prefer to do so mainly through prayer, giving, or even perhaps by going there yourself.

****

So, let us first discover where Hungary is on the modern map of Europe. It is in the middle of central Europe, more or less midway between the Baltic Sea to the north and the Adriatic Sea to the south, and therefore solidly landlocked. From its western frontier with Austria - to many of us its best-known neighbour - and skirting round its borders in a clockwise direction, we nowadays find Slovakia, followed by a short frontier with western Ukraine, then a long border with Rumania, before shorter ones again with Serbia (the dominant partner in the now-shrunken Yugoslavia), Croatia and finally Slovenia. All these have played some part in Hungary's past. However, as we shall see later, it has specially strong ties with the four countries from Slovakia to the north and Serbia to the south. These include the regions affected most by that notorious Treaty of Trianon which we encountered in the quiz.

A glance at a relief map of central Europe, that is to say one which contours and colours the land according to its height above sea level, would reveal that Hungary is the lowest country in the entire region. Indeed, it is one of the lowest in the entire continent. It embraces some of the foothills of the Alps to the west, and the Carpathian Mountains to the north and east, but most of its own territory is low and flat, or at most gently undulating. Its highest point (Mt. Kékestető, as we saw in Chapter 1), barely rises over 3000 feet above sea level, while much of Hungary stands below 500 feet.

The great River Danube, such an important 'dustless highway' as the German poet Holdenlin once famously described it, links Austria in the west and the Black Sea far away to the east. The Danube forms Hungary's north western border until it swings sharply southwards, thereafter bisecting the country into eastern and western halves. But we also find a sash-like band of mostly lowish, rolling hills lying diagonally across the country, separating the 'Small Plain' (in Hungarian, the *Kisalföld*) in the north west, from the 'Large Plain' (the *Nagyalföld*) in the south and east. Mt. Kékestető and Hungary's other highest hills are embedded in the north east section of that upland belt.

The soils of the plains are mostly very fertile and sustain profitable agriculture, though in some patches they are light and sandy and liable to wind erosion. I recall several times when driving was difficult because of miniature sandstorms in these areas! Also, parts of the eastern plains are so dry that their vegetation resembles that of the short grass prairies of North America. They are widely grazed by sheep, cattle and horses. all concerns of the famous *csikos*, 'cowboys' who nowadays dress in their traditional costumes only to perform for tourists.

So the Hungary which first captivated me in the mid-1960s, but to which - remarkably - I was not to return again until the mid-1990s, is mainly a land of wide, flat horizons subject to subtle interplays of light and shade. It has dark earth and pale earth;

sombre forests and glistening spinneys; large, bright stands of wheat and dull expanses of maize; variegated vegetable crops and flamboyant fields of golden sunflowers; as well as deep green waters fringed by waving reed beds and afloat with white and yellow rafts of verdant water lilies. Many of these foreground features are back-dropped by blue-grey, shadowy hills.

In essence this is still a quiet, shy countryside. It is all the lovelier because it contrasts so sharply with the nation's capital, Budapest. This large cosmopolitan metropolis apart, Hungary's cities and towns are compact, and rural population densities generally low. This is most obvious at night. Hence, as on the way to Kiskőrös in the previous chapter, it can be eerily possible to drive for many miles without catching a glimpse of a single light.

Budapest itself is, of course, in a league entirely of its own. Over two and a half million people, nearly one-third of the nation's population, live in the 'Greater Budapest' region. After it, the next biggest cities like Debrecen boast populations of no more than about 150,000 inhabitants at most. So the capital dominates the country in many different ways, and has life-styles unmatched elsewhere in the nation. Budapest also has Hungary's only commercial airport, Ferihegy - and virtually all its traffic jams. Yet even here the pace of life is more measured than in most Western European towns and cities.

Many of the fringe activities which absorb so much of our own time are engaged in much less by folk in Hungary, for the national average wage is still very low by our standards, and not much is left after payment has been made for housing, food, clothing and other everyday necessities. And as we shall see later this all affects church life too... and therefore the types of help from us that Hungarian Believers currently appreciate the most.

****

Now we have learnt a little about the land of Hungary today, we may turn back the clock and sketch how the nation has come about. We must also see why it is less than half the size it was less than a century ago. Many Hungarians now find themselves on the wrong sides of modern borders. One significant result of this is that our efforts to help Hungarian people and churches must be directed not at just one country, but towards at least five.

The oldest known human artefacts found in Hungary itself are said to date from many centuries before the time of Jesus Christ. However, it was not until a few centuries after His day that people who left legacies of any real importance began arriving in this region. Because Hungary is crossed by a major river system whose mainstream forms a natural route way across eastern Europe, and whose broad plains are much easier to farm than the high mountains of neighbouring countries, wave after wave of semi-nomadic immigrants have washed across it, mostly from the east. Some of these came from what we now call European Russia, but others were from far beyond that, even deep into central Asia. Still others were from regions east of the Black Sea, or south of the Caspian. Many of these were Magyars, from whom the classic Hungarians of today are descended. Hence the Hungarian's own name for Hungary is to us the tongue-twisting *Magyarország*, literally the 'Land of the Magyars'. Indeed, the Huns, after whom we wrongly choose to label their country in English, were earlier settlers of whom there are apparently very few, if any traces now.

With the influx of the Magyars came one of the most unique and distinctive languages in the world. Linguists tell us that the nearest relatives of the Hungarian language are apparently Finnish and Mongolian - and it takes an expert to spot the supposed similarities even with that far flung pair. To all practical intents and purposes Hungarians live on their own linguistic island, surrounded by a sea of Germanic, Slavic and Latin-type languages, and having nothing in common with any of them.

As the skirmishing Magyar invaders gradually became more settled in the Danube basin, opportunities for proper law and order grew. The key date, which is taken as the birth-date of Hungary, is the unusually easy-to-remember 1000 AD. This was when one tribal leader was able to establish authority over a much wider tribal area than his predecessors had. This leader came to be known as King István (Steven) 1. Unfortunately, periods of wars and invasions did not stop with his accession. Indeed, they were to be common features of life over the whole Hungarian region for most of the next millennium. History books detail these, so we need not.

However, two or three episodes were so important that they deserve a mention.

One of these was the Turkish occupation, from the Fifteenth to late Seventeenth Centuries. The Turks have left a legacy of heroic resistance stories, plus a few architectural fossils, though little else, and certainly no lasting religious complications.

The second of those particularly important periods yielded the united Austro-Hungarian Empire of the Eighteenth, and first half of the Nineteenth Centuries. Then, for better or for worse, Hungarian independence was at last restored again in 1849.

More recently Hungary has suffered horribly on account of World Wars 1 and 2. Mainly because of old ties with the German-speaking region through the lengthy union with Austria, Hungarians found themselves on the wrong sides in both world wars. Thus their beloved country was to be hard hit not only during those conflicts themselves, but even more so afterwards.

Following the end of World War 1, an international conference was held in Paris to review all the frontiers of middle Europe. This was to prove a vain attempt to prevent any further warfare. The resulting Treaty of Trianon, signed near Versailles, France on 4 July 1920, was devastating for Hungary and Hungarians alike. It is still bitterly resented today. What is its legacy? A Hungary which is <u>less than half the size it was</u> <u>before</u>, as Maps 1 and 2 clearly show. It still excludes many of the Hungarian people living in the region. The main areas lost to other countries - some of them entirely new creations - are present-day Slovakia to the north; the western corner of Ukraine in the north-east; the province of Vojvodina in northern Serbia to the south-east; and by far the worst loss of all, Transylvania to the east. This is now the western third of Rumania, a vast area of nearly 50,000 square miles (three-quarters the size of England), where in 1920 some two million Hungarians lived. In all these lost provinces the Hungarian language is still spoken by many people, including most of the large remaining ethnic Hungarian groups. We have found that many of our friends in Hungary today have relatives in one or more of these next-door neighbour nations, and visit them when they can.

Not surprisingly in view of all of this, there are also many Hungarian-speaking churches in these other states. One is the group of Hungarian Baptist churches in and around Pacir in northern

Serbia, to which Gillian and I sent clothing and other aid in January 2002. Many other fellowships are bilingual, regularly holding their services in two languages. One example of a bilingual church is the Baptist Church in Komarno, Slovakia, directly across the Danube from Komárom, of which more will be said in Chapters 3 and 4. Before 1920, Komárom and Komarno were northern and southern sectors of one single Hungarian city. Now Komarno is in a different country, and close relatives are separated from one another not only by the mile-wide river but also by fully-fledged customs and immigration controls.

So, this particular bit of history involving the Treaty of Trianon is clearly more important than most, even for any organisation like '4H' seeking to help Hungarians. If such help were targeted on present day Hungary alone, many other Hungarians would feel forgotten and neglected, indeed even more so than their motherland has been in Christian circles generally. Like many minority populations all over the world, the Hungarian *diaspora* are often looked down upon by their host nations on account of their different culture, customs and language. They rather rightly believe that they are not properly understood. Nor do they always enjoy adequate civil rights.

As Romans 12:1-8 insists, all Christians have a special responsibility to support and encourage fellow Believers less well positioned than themselves. Hence the precise title of this book. It is not *Helping HIS Heroes in Hungary*, but *Helping HIS Hungarian Heroes* - wherever they may live in central or eastern Europe. Our clear calling from the Lord is simply to 'help Hungarians'. Yes, most of them are in modern day Hungary, but many more are elsewhere and new doors are opening to help more of them too. for which they and we should all be glad.

****

Our next ventures into what has shaped the Hungarian world as we see it at the beginning of the Twenty-first Century concerns the history of the Christian faith among these people, and some of the main threats to faith which have arisen from time to time. These were particularly strong from the end of the Second World War until about 1990.

King István 1 assumed widespread power in 1000 AD. One of the most important international leaders to whom he turned for recognition as king was Pope Sylvester in Rome. Thus, István's coronation on Christmas Day 1000 was as a Christian king. Thereafter the work of Catholic missionaries, first invited into Hungary by István's father, Prince Géza, expanded rapidly. Catholicism remains the most widely held faith in Hungary today, though a lot of its adherents are quite nominal. Meanwhile, the Protestant Reformation influenced many in the Danube Basin from the Sixteenth Century on. The north-eastern regional capital, Debrecen became a focus of Calvinism, and the site of a Reformed College. This is still functioning today, over 400 years afterwards. Even a brief Counter Reformation waged by the Catholic Church with some unlikely help from the then occupying Turks could not dim the new, clearer light of the rediscovered Gospel. Thus, almost as many Hungarians - if pressed by us today - would claim allegiance to Calvinist or Lutheran creeds as others do to Catholic dogma. Generally speaking, Protestants are more numerous to the east of the Danube, and Catholics to the west.

From the early Twentieth Century powerful and sinister non-Christian forces then began to arrange themselves against the message of the Bible until, in 1942, a communist government took control of the country. The next era, which was to become so bleak for so many, was ushered in with strong backing from the old Soviet Union. Describing that time the reliable and widely praised *Rough Guide to Hungary* succinctly says that:

> *"Church schools were seized, Cardinal Mindszenty* (head of the Catholic Church in Hungary and therefore the most high-profile Christian of that period) *was jailed for 'espionage', and the peasants were forced into collective farms. More than 500,000 Hungarians (five percent of the population) were imprisoned, tortured or shot in concentration camps like Recsk* (see Chapter 1), *or were deported to the Soviet Union - victims of the AVH secret police who spread terror throughout society."*

All sections of Hungarian life were to be deeply affected by the new regime for, as the *Rough Guide* continues:

"Under the (first) Five Year Plan, heavy industry took absolute priority over agriculture and consumer production. To fill the new factories, country dwellers streamed into the towns and women were dragooned into the labour force. Living standards plummeted, and everyone was subjected to the laws and dictates of the (Communist) Party. 'Class conscious' workers and peasants were raised to high positions, and 'class enemies' were discriminated against, while Party officials enjoyed luxuries unavailable to the rest of the populace, who suffered hunger and squalor."

Some aspects of my own first visit to Hungary in 1965, attending that Summer School in Hungarian Language and Culture in Debrecen, have been described in the opening chapter of this book. Remember, I was quickly made aware of some of the dangers a totalitarian state posed for individuals who tried to follow Jesus Christ. Despite every assertion to the contrary, the communist era was dreadfully difficult for Christians and their churches. Many places of worship were forced to close, and church-owned land and buildings confiscated by the state. Services in the remaining churches were hedged around with restrictions, and open-air events were banned. Sunday Schools were forbidden too - hence the fact that so-called children's 'Bible Circles', which were sometimes permitted by communist local authorities. are more common even to this very day. Christian publishing, beginning with the Bible, was proscribed for many years, and Christians often featured among the half-a-million folk from Hungary alone who were exiled or executed because their personal beliefs were considered threats to the new atheistic regime.

Of course, many Hungarians suffered similarly in those neighbouring countries which had not lost, but gained, land and people under the Treaty of Trianon. The adjacent countries of Czechoslovakia, Rumania, Yugoslavia, and Ukraine (as part of the Union of Soviet Socialist Republics) were also controlled by communists for most of the second half of the Twentieth Century.

The first half of Pálma's poem at the end of the previous chapter provides one small glimpse of what life was like for Christian leaders across this whole region while the communists were in power. Everyone who was a Believer during that period has his or her own tales to tell of hardships they had to face because of their faith in Jesus Christ. Most particularly this was true of the pastors like

Pálma's Dad, and theological students training for the ministry. Help from the West, usually provided through those brave people, had to be delivered with great care and sensitivity. This is why Pálma's poetic friends were ones whose: '...*faces were familiar*', but whose: '...*names were not known*'. The welcome Western guests would usually pass over the Bibles they had brought, plus little personal gifts under cover of darkness. Yes, they were eager to avoid police even if - occasionally! - those servants of the state innocently tried to be helpful, for example by offering directions if ever the visitors were temporarily unsure of the way.

The son of one senior pastor recalls how the Bibles they received from the UK would always be quickly bricked up behind a false wall in their garage until, a few at a time, they could be distributed near and far.

Many another story of such danger, bravery and hardship could be shared, but a lot have been retold elsewhere and the purpose of this account is different: to put such situations into a wider historical perspective. And it should never be forgotten that, as throughout the whole of the old communist world the Hungarian Church came to be refined by its privations, just as the New Testament Church did as described by Peter in his First Epistle. However, many Hungarian Believers have also remarked with justification that they came to suffer not just a 'little', but a LOT!

So, how did the harsh Hungarian communist regime finally come to an end? For a few prematurely heady days in late October 1956 - echoing similarly short-lived periods of hope in Poland to the north - it had seemed that general resentment of the oppressive dictatorial government in Budapest might have seen it brushed away after less than a single uncomfortable decade. During the last part of that crucial month, *AVH* guards opened fire with tragic consequences on unarmed demonstrating crowds. At that point even units of the Hungarian army began siding with the protestors, against Soviet forces stationed in their country. A subsequent partial withdrawal of Russian troops was negotiated for 29 October 1956, but that was merely a delaying tactic on the part of their High Command in Moscow. So, on 4 November, Budapest suddenly found itself surrounded by Soviet tanks newly bent on business, whilst more armour poured back into the country from the east. Despite fierce battles, not only in the capital but also in Debrecen and other important cities, the outcome was never in any doubt. Quickly communism reasserted its harsh control, its leaders now prepared to do whatever it took to assert complete power and authority over the common people. Thereafter 'The Party' was to remain in charge for more than another thirty years.

In the meantime, many who had fought so bravely for their nation's freedom during that unforgettable two-week period of heady hope in the autumn of 1956 fled to the West, fearing that they would be captured, tortured and even killed if they did not escape. Over one-fifth of a million somehow managed to cross the minefields into Austria - the only non-communist country with which Hungary had a common frontier. One of those who escaped in this way was the Josef we will meet again in Chapter 3. Now back in the country of his birth as an ordained evangelist, he was first to endure a tough life in England with many a personal problem before his mid-life conversion in the 1980s. Josef's dramatic personal story has been told more fully in *Scientists Who Find God.*. Suffice it to say here that many Hungarians in Western Europe, North America, Australia and elsewhere who are now in their 60s or older left their homeland at the same time as Josef as the 1956 uprising was cruelly squashed. They have their own hair-raising stories to tell of life-threatening situations during the uprising, as well as of border crossing perils, refugee camp miseries and resettlement difficulties, plus the added pain of having to live far away from relatives and other loved ones for the next 35 years or more.

Mercifully, when the end of communist rule finally came in Hungary it did so with a proverbial whimper rather than another bang. Indeed, softening had already begun to be evident in some areas of official policy a few years before the change to democracy came around 1990. For example in the mid-1980s it was fascinating and encouraging to hear that the Hungarian Parliament had passed a brand new decree concerning the Bible. This book, so long an object of its dislike and distrust, was now to be read and taught in the nation's schools! The official reason for such an amazing turnaround was this: "So much Hungarian history, literature, art and architecture cannot be understood without a knowledge of the Bible." Whatever the reason, the Holy Spirit was clearly at work.

Many marvelled at the time, and wondered what further miracles God might have in store across the whole communist region of

Europe and Asia in the years ahead. However, as with most prayer-answering miracles in Bible times, what happened next was to be: *"immeasurably more than all we ask or even imagine "* (Ephesians 3:20). Despite the plethora of prayers for freedom for Believers under communism to live and work openly for the Lord without fear of persecution, or even worse, most of us who prayed had little confidence that God would really hear and answer us. And very few of us, if any, expected that He would do so in the dramatic and conclusive fashion that was to follow!

At times I have spoken in public concerning the end of the communist era. This finally unfolded before the eyes of the world on TV, night after night as amazing scenes from one country after another were beamed around the globe. I have suggested that what took place was an epic event, on a par with major ones in Bible times. To my way of thinking these include such astonishing happenings as the escape of the Israelites from Egypt across the Red Sea in the Old Testament, and the spread of the early Church in the New Testament. And I shall always consider such parallels are apt.

In Hungary itself, the end of communism was so orderly that it could scarcely be called a revolution, except that the changes that followed have been totally revolutionary. Again to cut a long story short, there was to be virtually no loss of life along Hungary's road to free elections, and in 1990 a centre-right coalition was democratically swept to power to govern the nation.

Elsewhere in the Hungarian world the end of communist rule did not everywhere work out as painlessly as it did in Hungary. Slovakia and Ukraine managed to avoid bloodshed too, but the post-communist revolution against President Ceaucescu in Rumania was terrible not only for him but also for many Rumanian citizens, including those of Hungarian descent. Interestingly it was a Hungarian pastor, László Tőkés, in the Transylvanian city of Timisoara who was generally recognised as the key instigator of the Rumanian uprising. However, Rumania's path to democracy, and more recently towards a Western-style market economy, has proved much more difficult than that of its own next door neighbour to the west.

Elsewhere, Yugoslavia to the south contorted itself through a whole series of death-pang civil wars, and Serbia, the centrepiece of the old Federal Republic, was sorely inflicted with President

Milosevic's infamous policy of 'ethnic cleansing'. Through this he tried to forcibly remove non-Serb people groups from his shrinking state. After fighting fruitless wars with other former parts of Yugoslavia - Croatia and Bosnia-Hercegovina - and even losing the north western province of Slovenia without a fight. Milosevic tried to remove the majority population of Albanians from Kosovo in the south. After that he was expected to turn his attention to Hungarians in Vojvodina in the north, but mercifully the United Nations intervened before this could begin in earnest.

However, many Hungarians and others living in Vojvodina in the middle to late 1990s decided it would be prudent to leave Serbia while they could do so voluntarily, and did so in their thousands. Crossing the southern Hungarian border, they became refugees seeking asylum. As we will see later, many found themselves temporarily in an old Russian army camp in the town of Bicske, just west of Budapest. Though Milosevic is no longer in power, and at the time of writing is being tried for war crimes in The Netherlands, the lot of the remaining Hungarian population in Vojvodina is still less than completely happy. Help for this, and especially its Christian community, is another current priority.

In the mid-1990s, Hungary became a member of NATO. It is also one of the aspiring new members of the European Union for admission in 2004. We pray for the day when this happens, for border crossings from Austria can still be long and tedious, and Customs controls can still try the patience of saints! On entry into the European Union such problems will become things of the past. How glad we will be when the testings and tensions they have caused will be no more than fading memories - though again we will never forget many associated instances of gloriously surprising and liberating grace!

Gillian, for example, never did forget the eight-hour delay she, David and Peter once had to endure at the Hegyeshalom crossing from Austria into Hungary as recently as 1995. They were transporting nothing more sinister than a cargo of used clothing, shoes, toys - and a boxful of toothbrushes as Chapter 3 will explain.

Seven years later, in May 2002 I myself, along with friends in Hungary, wasted many hours, and even days, trying to secure the release from Customs of a much smaller consignment of one hundred kilos of clothing, books, papers and other largely personal effects. These had been sent out on a regular freight service, free of charge through the help of a Methodist friend who works at a depot in Avonmouth. In the end all were finally pronounced Customs cleared - some three months after they had crossed the Austro-Hungarian frontier! At times like these I have had ample cause to recall a wry email I once received from Dan, an American missionary friend working with the International Church in Budapest: *"Life in Hungary is great, so long as you do not want to buy a house... or have anything to do with Hungarian Customs!"*

****

"But how then," you may ask, "has all this: 'Where, When and What of the Hungarian World' influenced the way things are today?" Last of all in this background chapter we turn to matters of contemporary church life, then finally to attitudes to spiritual things among those who are not yet Christians.

As in many other countries, churches in Hungary bear a variety of different labels. These can be simultaneously both helpful and misleading. We have seen that the Catholic Church is still the biggest in early Twenty-first Century Hungary. Much of its membership is very nominal, though some Catholics - like several students I quickly came to appreciate so much in the University of Veszprém in March 2003 - clearly know and love the Lord. Also, it has scarcely grown since 1990. The Lutheran and Calvinist Churches are not far behind in terms of their combined membership. However, as with Anglicans in the UK, their churches vary greatly from place to place. Much depends on whether the local pastor is a real Bible-believing Christian or not, and whether there is a local evangelical tradition. Other denominational groups are smaller, but some have grown encouragingly in recent years. These include Baptists, Evangelicals, Pentecostals and Charismatics, whose combined forces are much more numerous than in Poland, for example, but much less so than in next-door Rumania where the evangelical tradition in general has been stronger, and where much more help has been forthcoming from the West.

There are relatively few 'big' churches with congregations of a few hundred or so, but many 'small' churches attended by a handful or two of faithful folk, many of whom are elderly. Quite a lot of children may attend special events like Holiday Bible Clubs, and in the livelier churches good numbers of young people are real source of encouragement. In these respects, therefore, the pattern of actively evangelising, Bible-believing fellowships is quite like that here at home in the UK. However, one significant difference is that in most Hungarian congregations there are fewer-than-needed members in their middle years, especially men. This last fact has not helped church growth or church planting since the end of communism, for church and congregational leadership comes most naturally from that group. Also, the scarceness of middle-aged men means that in some places church fabric maintenance and new building projects are hard even to contemplate. This is one reason why we ourselves in recent years have put so much store on taking Practical Mission Teams to Hungary, as Chapter 4 will recount in much more greater detail.

"So, why are middle-aged church members so rare?" you may legitimately ask. The answer is mainly because of the intense propaganda against the Church and the Gospel all the way from the late 1940s to the late 1980s. That unrelenting propaganda and the severe personal pressures that accompanied it weighed most heavily upon the young people of the day. We recognise that across most of the world it is in their teens that most who come to faith in God find Him. Thus it is no surprise that in today's church memberships there are now a couple of generations in which the Christian faith is quite strongly under-represented. This, in its turn, puts extra pressure on the mums and dads and grandparents who did trust Jesus Christ in the 'Old Days' days, for more responsibilities rest on their shoulders than would normally have been the case.

To make matters even worse, Hungary's economy has been depressed by the end of communism and the collapse of COMECON, the trading block which used to link eastern European countries with the old Soviet Union. Thus, jobs are still too few, and wages too low to ensure that everyone can enjoy a reasonable standard of living. This has had particularly serious implications for charitable institutions like churches. One result is that these have few resources which can be spent on the fabric and fittings of their buildings, great though the need for updating these may be. Also, few fellowships are able to pay their pastors, most of whom must therefore work to keep the proverbial wolf from their family door.

This is why a high proportion of pastors over the eastern half of our continent are what we term 'lay pastors', even those who have two, three or even more congregations to lead.

So how do Hungarian churches generally cope with the challenges facing them today? In some ways very well. One thing which has greatly impressed me is how many of the evangelical churches serve as foci for everyday family activity. These churches are open most hours of the week, whereas their British counterparts are usually closed. Vital work maintaining and cleaning church premises is usually done not by a caretaker or two but by many friends after work, with Dad making essential repairs to the structure while Mum is busy with a mop and bucket. Their children do their homework in the Sunday School room, or play inside or out depending on the season of the year. In many of the smaller towns and villages churches have gardens where children safely amuse themselves, mainly with basic, natural 'toys' like sticks, stones, sand and water. But they are perfectly content with them....

Thus there is a close community spirit at the heart of many fellowships, where individual families merge to become one bigger, truly happy family, sharing many of each other's concerns as well as each other's joys and blessings. And even younger children seem to understand it is best to put the Lord and the needs of His work first. While working with one of our Practical Teams at the Baptist Church in Komárom, we found towards the end of the week that our joint budget for materials had all been spent - but a little more sand was needed to finish some rendering. Sándor, the lay evangelist had been temporarily living with his wife Ággie and children Rébékah and Bence in the children's ministry room in the church while a long-delayed flat was being slowly prepared for them elsewhere. Thinking about the need for a few more bucketfuls of sand, Sándor suddenly had a bright idea.

"There's enough in the children's sandpit over there," he exclaimed, pointing to a little play area beloved by Rébékah and her young friends. Home made, it was fashioned from an old truck tyre full of builder's sand.

Asking one of our men to bring a shovel, Sándor picked up a pail and motioned us to follow him over to that place where Rébékah was playing. Sándor gave his daughter a brief explanation. Next minute her playstuff began to disappear. One of the many telling memories I have of church life in Hungary then ensued: far from complaining, or trying to resist the removal of 'her' sand, little Rébékah began to help, filling her own tiny bucket with some of it, and emptying it into her father's much bigger one....

It is said in another context in the Old Testament that: *"A little child shall lead them"* (Isaiah 11:6). How well that comment could have applied to Rébékah's selfless action! I resolved at the time that one thing I should try to do back home in the future was to raise help for churches like the one at Komárom to provide better play areas for the Hungarian church children. Many like Rébékah and her friends spend so much time in them in the long summer evenings and at weekends.

****

It is time to draw this chapter to a close. In it, in our attempt to scene-set for the chapters which follow, we have covered many centuries and quite a lot of ground. Here is a factual framework for our future prayers for Hungary and certain of its neighbours.

In conclusion, it should be stressed that all Hungarian Bible-believing churches are still savouring today the delights of freedoms which were denied them for so long. However, adjusting to the present age of opportunity is easier for younger people than it can be for many who are older. In particular it has proved difficult for some of the older church leaders and members to adjust their outlooks and ways of doing things to take advantage of the new situation, for many of them lived all their Christian lives under the severe constraints of communism. Thus, leadership is passing perhaps more quickly than it otherwise might have done to younger men and women in their twenties and thirties. This 'young guard' is excitedly and energetically organising everything from Bible and church-planting conferences to tent missions and special Gospel outreach events of kinds that we in the West may even think have become 'out-of-date'.

Above all we see there is a happiness to be able to spend much time with other Believers, on church premises and on the Lord's business. But most Hungarian fellowships are so short of financial resources that there is little they can do unaided to improve those premises and make them better suited to the beginning of the

Twenty-first Century. Whatever they can do is done with real dedication, pride and pleasure, but there are many ways in which we can help them to do more.

In the meantime, they seem to have a much greater confidence in the Gospel and its power to transform lives than we often demonstrate ourselves. One particular way in which this is evident is through their ready use of resource materials, advertising campaigns and the media to let their whole communities know what they are doing, and why.

"We have good news that people so desperately need," they say. "It is such a <u>tremendous blessing</u> to know the Lord that we must do ALL WE CAN to share it with others too. For many years in our part of the world we had to do so mostly in secret - but now it is <u>wonderful</u> because we can live OPENLY for the Lord...!"

CHAPTER 3

TOOTHBRUSHES, TEDDY BEARS AND MANY OTHER THINGS

Why photograph toothbrushes?!

Escorted by Hungarian-born evangelist Josef and his English wife Wendy, we approached the entrance of the massive grey building in subdued mood. Until a few years earlier it had been an officers' training school for the Hungarian Army. It still had a regimental air, despite having become one of the largest children's homes in the whole of Hungary - though not strictly an 'orphanage' as some still call it, because many of the children living there were and are not true orphans. Rather, many are boys and girls unwanted by their parents. On that first visit of ours in the mid-1990s there were many children in the Kőszeg Home near the border with Austria who had come into the care of the state under the pre-communist government. In that era anyone not wanting their offspring for any reason at all could hand them over to a state institution to do their parenting for them....

In the early 1990s many a scandalous situation had been discovered in similar state 'orphanages' in other eastern bloc countries - and revealed in all their horror to the rest of the dazed world through the media, especially TV. Thus it was with some relief that Gillian and I found that conditions in Kőszeg were bad enough to warrant any positive response we might be able to mobilise, but not so bad as to deeply shock. We were to leave the Home concerned and thoughtful, rather than very angry or despairing.

But what exactly did we find? ·

The building itself was clearly in quite urgent need of repair both inside and out. Many of its former function rooms were being used as dormitories, complete with makeshift platforms to provide two-tiered sleeping accommodation for extra children. At that time some 600 called that place their home. The sleeping platforms, we were told, had been made with timber from trees cut from the surrounding woods. Elsewhere, in former corridors where second levels could not easily be added, old tubular metal-framed beds were packed so close together that it would have been impossible for the teenagers who slept in them to reach their own beds without scrambling over those of others. There was no room for little luxuries like individual bedside cabinets, lights or lockers.

Schoolrooms were amazing time warps, living memories of those at home in the UK 50 years or more before, complete with tidy rows of wooden desks with inkwells, sloping, lidded book compartments, and integral bench-style seats. The classrooms contained no evidence of special teaching resources or visual aids apart from things the children themselves had produced. Computers and their associated paraphernalia - now standard in UK schools - were conspicuous by their total absence. Clearly 'talk and chalk' still reigned in Kőszeg.

However, of all the parts of the building we were allowed to visit, the worst by far were the washroom and toilet blocks. Underfoot, water from leaky pipes was everywhere. Despite the efforts of bare-footed children struggling with mops to lower the water levels on the floors, this stubbornly remained virtually ankle deep.

But two things encouraged us. One was that although the children looked thin, and clearly had few clothes or things to play with, they looked reasonably well and happy. More than that, it was obvious from the staff we met that they were caring people - unlike many given media attention in other parts of eastern Europe - and were doing the very best they could with the limited resources at their disposal to serve the children well. Indeed they themselves despaired that they could do no more. They had such paltry budgets with which to work.

One unforgettable statistic was provided by the young assistant director who was showing us around: "Each year," she mourned, "we have just 4000 forints (in 1995 about £15) for each child for all his or her clothing and footwear needs!"

I thought immediately how hard it was to buy more than one quite average shirt for that amount, or maybe an average tie... and how difficult it had been to encourage our own children to wear a pair of trainers that cost that amount or less. A single pair that carried the 'street cred' of a 'designer label' cost far more than that.

The assistant director continued: "We hear of convoys of aid that pass through the border crossing just up the road, on their way to Rumania, Ukraine or Yugoslavia - but no-one has helped us here. WE'RE PRAYING THAT A TRUCK WILL BREAK DOWN NEARBY so that we can have some help here too!"

Long before Gillian and I returned home from that brief visit to Hungary - the first I had paid there for 30 years since the Summer School in Debrecen described in Chapter 1 - we had come to a significant conclusion. No-one should ever have to pray that someone else must suffer in order that others might benefit, however deep their need! Something must be organised to ensure that a truck would not have to break down so that at least some token aid could reach Kőszeg's Children's Home.

An outline of what happened next has been described already by Gillian and myself in Chapter 10 of the recent SGA book: *Glimpses of God's Grace**. It is worth excerpting from it here:

"Through that winter we said: 'Yes, please!' whenever anyone offered us new, or good used clothing, shoes, bed linen and toys. And with virtually no effort on our part, word as to what we wanted seemed to get around.

"By March 1996 we had enough goods stacked in our garage and the front room of a nearby friendly farm to fill the 'Luton-bodied' Transit van loaned to us, and insured free of charge, by a well-known Somerset shoe manufacturing firm. On the long journey to Hungary our three drivers - Gillian, plus Peter and David from our church - found the Transit van would not go faster than 60 mph (downhill!), and sometimes would not reach 40 mph (uphill!). Thus four of the five days they were away were spent on the road. Excepting, that is, the eight agonising hours at the border east of Vienna - not trying to get into Hungary,

but for reasons of misplaced officiousness by fellow members of the European Union, *out of Austria!* After six of those eight hours the Transit crew had phoned to the UK and Hungary requesting urgent prayers - fearing they might have to turn round, and bring the whole load home again! Soon the prayers were answered, and the van made Györ just after midnight.

"The next day, though, when the crew took the Ford Transit for refuelling, it became clear that the Lord had answered prayers for problems unseen as well as seen, for they found it took 68.25 litres of gas to fill the tank. Thought-provokingly this was more than its capacity as stated in the maker's manual. Near midnight, on the last leg down a deserted motorway, the team had somehow continued travelling despite a bone-dry tank...!

"Afterwards the goods they carried were taken on to Kőszeg by Wendy and Josef to the general joy of all concerned. And there were at least two sequels worth noting briefly. One was that, as a result of this and other demonstrations of God's love and care for folk generally out of sight of society, Kőszeg Children's Home opened to the Gospel. Some of its teachers as well as children have since responded to the claims of Jesus Christ upon their lives.

"The second sequel has been in many ways more unexpected, and even more wide reaching. A few months after the delivery trip, Josef showed us some transparencies taken inside the Home.

"'Why ever did you take *this* one?" we enquired, mystified by a picture of a half-panelled wall. It was adorned only by a shelf, bearing a row of plastic mugs from which some toothbrushes poked.

"'Oh, didn't you know?' replied Josef, 'there was a box of about 300 toothbrushes on your van. The children were so thrilled that there were enough for one between two that they insisted that I took a picture of the toothbrushes, to specifically thank the people in the UK who had given them!'

Some months after that unique explanation, we were asked - for the first time ever - to address a Women's Institute meeting, in a village near Tiverton in Devon. That special Day Conference on Eastern Europe was attended by over 100 delegates from all over the county. Our brief was to talk about changes which had ensued in that region since the post-communist revolutions about 1990. Beginning (as requested) with news of the scientific scene, I talked also about social and economic conditions, and finally how, in many different ways, SGA's role in central and eastern Europe had changed too in response to new needs and opportunities. We felt glad when our encounter with such a formidable body of ladies ended, and we left unsure as to the kind of impact we had made. Indeed, I remember returning home thinking how odd and unrewarding public speaking can sometimes seem to be.

"A few days later, though, these thoughts were to be roundly rebuked. Gillian took the key phone call, from the organiser of the conference. Part of the conversation went like this:

"'We were specially touched by what your husband had to say about the Children's Home in Kőszeg.... We are wondering if you would like us to collect more toothbrushes for you to take. Our ladies are good at things like this!'

"'Oh well yes, that would be great,' Gillian replied, not noticing the slight stress Betty had placed on the word 'good'. But we were both curious to see if even toothbrushes could somehow be divinely used instruments of blessing....

"A couple of years later still we were absolutely sure they could. Very soon after that phone conversation, toothbrushes began to descend on us in droves - plus (for some reason not quite clear to us at the time, but welcome nonetheless), tubes of toothpaste, towels, flannels, and bars of soap in roughly equal measures: several thousand of each kind!

"So, kids in Kőszeg Children's Home came to enjoy cleaner teeth and healthier gums, plus many more folk elsewhere in Hungary...."

Happily, other help was quickly forthcoming for the Home in Kőszeg too. Much of it was organised by Josef and Wendy themselves, working hand-in-hand with the little Baptist home church in the town. Soon, other consignments of clothing, bedding and shoes arrived from the UK, and a work party from the English Midlands that helped correct some of the worst of the plumbing problems. Maybe it was such help from abroad that prompted the state authorities to further improve the orphanage themselves, so much so that by the turn of the century the premises had been largely renovated in several ways, and the number of children housed there considerably reduced.

Even more happily, links between the Home and the local Baptist church have grown and strengthened. Bible clubs for children wishing to attend have become popular, and as we have seen some children - and some of their teachers - have responded to the Gospel and put their faith in Jesus Christ.

Sometimes when Gillian and I thought of that initial aid delivery which we organised to Kőszeg with the help of many friends in south-west England we reflected on the basic similarity between toothbrushes and some types of old-type keys! For we have marvelled again and again that in God's hands even those humble oral hygiene implements can be used by Him to unlock doors previously shut fast to His people and His Word...!

From toiletries to teddy bears

In the years that immediately followed the toothbrush saga, other new doors for sharing the Gospel were also opened by such simple, everyday necessities, provided through the generosity of the Devon Women's Institutes and other friends.

Once the Kőszeg kids had been set up with a new toothbrush each, plus other toiletries, and the Home had been left stocks for the future, we assessed the assorted items remaining in our garage. There were a LOT! At a conservative estimate we could probably make up a further 2000 complete washkits from them - if we had enough new washbags. We had received relatively few of these receptacles from Devon, and all of them had gone to Kőszeg. So we set about acquiring more bags before asking ourselves the question: "How might we best use all the extra toiletry sets?"

From discussions with pastors in Hungary we were soon to glean some answers. Since 1990, many churches which for so long had been very heavily restricted in what they could do for others either spiritually or materially, have been revelling in their new-found freedom to show the love of the Lord to people in need. Thus, pastors eagerly accepted all the washkits we could offer, and used them in several imaginative ways. A few examples of these must suffice. In every case it has also been subsequently possible to share the Gospel with others too

Győr, the regional capital of north west Hungary, is a busy administrative centre of about 130,000 souls. One of its special institutions is the Mother-and-Baby Unit. Here many of the unmarried mums of the city and district are helped through the traumas of unplanned, unexpected and - in some cases at least - unwanted motherhood. Often they are completely unsupported by the fathers of the new little citizens they had helped bring into the world. To make matters worse, the post-communist Hungarian government is in no position financially to provide as much support as the former dictatorial administration could. Thus any help at all that can be given to those young mothers is almost literally worth its weight in gold. Gifts of washkits, modest though they may seem to us, have been accepted gratefully. This is not least because of the love, care and concern of which they speak. Győr's Morning Star Christian Ministry Centre, featured in Chapter 4, was the channel in this case, helping hapless girls find faith and hope for life.

Meanwhile, in the nearby country town of Pápa, some 30 or so miles away, where Josef and Wendy have successfully planted the new Cornerstone Church, the state-run Family Help Centre warmly welcomed supplies of washkits too, plus good quality used clothing, shoes and toys. All these and more have been shared among disadvantaged and hard-pressed people. On one unforgettable occasion Gillian and two men from a Team of ours working on the Morning Star were asked to accompany Josef and Wendy to give out some of the aid items we had brought by minibus from England. Clad in working clothes, and adorned by dust and emulsion paint instead of powder or after-shave, our workers were taken aback by the reception committee which awaited them in Pápa. This included the mayor, chief town councillor and head nurse of the Family Help Centre - plus, horror of horrors - a <u>television camera crew</u>! As Gillian explained afterwards, rarely can any televised presentation ceremony anywhere in Europe have involved such scruffily dressed stars!

But there was to be at least one satisfying sequel to that unexpectedly high profile, if not exactly high-fashion event. The chief nurse was so grateful for the little help we had been able to provide that she expressed the wish to come to the next meeting at Josef and Wendy's newly-planted little church. At that time it met in a room in the semi-detached house which one of our earlier Teams had helped prepare for that very purpose. That midweek meeting was unusual in two respects. Several of our current Team went over from Győr to participate. So, the main item on the programme came to be a video on hovercraft operations in far-away Papua New Guinea. This was introduced by our 'Number One' driver, Stephen, who would shortly be leaving Bristol for the notorious Fly River delta region of New Guinea. There he was to be one of the mechanics responsible for keeping two of those exotic vessels in working order throughout a Christian Hover Aid expedition.

The small audience for that video screening was soon totally engrossed, for even the Danube shrinks in comparison with the mighty Fly, especially in the region of its enormous estuary.

Furthermore, because Hungary is far inland, any images of the sea are viewed with special fascination. Finally, to our knowledge no hovercraft has ever visited that country, so Stephen's presentation about them could scarcely have been higher in novelty value.

Over coffee afterwards the chief nurse enthused: "If I had known the evening would be so good, I would have brought my son too!" - and began attending the church regularly forthwith. Soon she professed faith in Jesus Christ as her personal Saviour, and became a valued member of the growing Fellowship. Toothbrushes, you see, may not only help unlock doors for sharing the Gospel, but also hearts for accepting it....

And this is by no means the end of the washkit story. We have seen how, in the 1990s, Hungary's economy dipped alarmingly as its ties with COMECON, the old eastern European international trading bloc headed by the former Soviet Union were cut to shreds. Thereafter, creating a wholly new type of economic structure in the region would prove to be a long and painful process. This is by no means ended yet. When gifts are given in Hungary, say at birthdays or for Christmas, it remains true that the more practical they are, the better!

Thus, many of the washkits have been given away by churches in north-west Hungary in connection with church planting, where special efforts are always made to make new friends in the local community. Summer evangelism is another context in which they have been very useful too, for example as prizes for children attending events in the 'Baptist Tent', which is deployed each year in a well-planned sequence of towns and cities across the nation.

Meanwhile, at home in the UK I treasure a little set of carefully crafted, brightly coloured, crepe paper flowers. These were given to Gillian and me in return for a sack of washkits taken to a playschool in Győr. During our visit several groups of the most endearing little children imaginable treated their special guests from England to traditional Hungarian nursery rhymes and engaging dance routines.

Those tiny poppets were also the first to receive some of the many hand-knitted teddy bears which had unexpectedly yet usefully arrived at our home with another consignment of toothbrushes, toothpaste, talc and other toiletries from the wonder collectors of the Women's Institutes in Devon. Simply shaped, yet soft and with appealing, sympathetic faces and lovely cheerful clothes, these woollen bears have since brought happiness to literally hundreds of Hungarian homes - into which they have also carried news of local church activities, and invitations to whole families to attend each and every one of these.

Recently the supply of toiletries to us has dried up, and all our stocks have gone. However, without our asking, knitted teddies continue to be handed to us from time to time, from different sources, including folk who have never given us anything before. For children of some ages they are among the best types of gifts they could possibly be given: warm, cuddly expressions of the love God has in His heart for everyone.

So we are grateful to all who have lent a hand with any of these things, particularly friends who have spent much time, effort and money in the process, maybe even in particularly unexpected ways

. One day I took a phone call from a dear Jamaican couple in Bristol whom I have known for several years. Knowing our need for more washbags, they invited us to collect some they had just made. On arriving at their house we found they had half-a-dozen large, overflowing boxes of them to give us. Each box was full of colourful, neatly machined bags, complete with handy drawstring tops.

"However many are there?" I gasped when I saw them first.

"Oh, about 700, my dears," came the smiling reply.

"But Esme, your eye is still so sore from your cataract operation! However did you manage all that sewing?"

Esme's response was one I will never forget. Perhaps it could even be an inspiration to menfolk who possess under-used or even suppressed gifts, talents or serving opportunities of kinds traditionally reserved for ladies: "Oh, my dears, but it wasn't _me_ who did them - it was JACK!"

Many other things

With the passage of time, and for many different reasons, the practical aid we have organised for Hungarians has recently become more and more varied, and targeted in a widening range of different directions. In many cases though, this has happened because of things we have been offered rather than things we ourselves have set out to collect. For years, rather than advertising the need for any special type of 'aid', if offered anything my policy has been to say: "Yes, please!" God understands much better than any of us what is currently needed, and would be useful. Thus, in the light of our limited ability to take or send bulky items to 'the field', time after time His plans have truly proved to be perfect.

One example of an unexpected item offered to Gillian and myself which now has an appropriate new home was detailed in Chapter 16 of *Glimpses of God's Grace* - an English pastor's briefcase. Originally owned by a leading English evangelical minister, this is now giving equally valuable service to Pastor Zsolt in Tatabánya, Hungary.

Then there was the instance of the electronic keyboard offered Gillian by her brother John. This, after some repairs, was just the job for Pastor János in Győr. His two girls had recently begun piano lessons, but had nothing to practice on in their family's three-roomed apartment. We learned later that the keyboard was also being pressed into service for midweek meetings in their church.

I also vividly remember the hydraulic hoist we were enabled by friends to buy cheaply in Bristol from an understanding 'mobility apparatus centre', and the excitement and gratitude shown by Pastor Attila and his wife Erzsébét when they first saw it. The substantial gift of money that permitted the purchase was from a lady we had met but once. Attila and Erzsébét's son is brain damaged due to oxygen starvation at birth, and has only half the normal brain capacity. As a result of this he is severely spastic. Nonetheless he is much loved by all the members of his family, who are trying to look after him at home despite the strain this places on their health, strength and resources. Pastor Attila has twice recently lost jobs with engineering firms because of their bankruptcies. Today he is - moderately! - glad to have work as an assistant chimney sweep. But the family budget, always tight, is under great strain on account of little Donát's very disabling condition. As Donát has grown bigger it has become all the more difficult for his slightly built mum to lift him. There have been times when we have been in their home and she has been suffering from abdominal strain caused in that way.

Back in 1996 we detached three men for two days from one of our working groups based elsewhere to lay a concrete path from the road outside Donát's home. This was so that his pushchair could be wheeled all the way to the door without getting bogged down in the muddy patch that was there before. Then, in 2001 it was such a pleasure to be able to give the family the hydraulic hoist, so that Donát could be moved from bed to push chair and then into the bath without having to be lifted manually. And how pleased we had been to be able to take it out as part of our normal baggage allowance on our flights from Bristol to Budapest via Amsterdam! The hoist, when packed, was so bulky that we had to get special approval from the airline to take it. We knew it would be quite heavy too, so we took the precaution of removing the heaviest single part of it, the hydraulic cylinder, to take in our carry-on luggage. It was fortunate that this was not weighed... though I think my arms were stretched a bit even when just lifting it on and off the baggage trolleys!

Even more unexpected gifts: 'for the work in Hungary' have sometimes included many items at once, not just one or two. A South Gloucestershire friend asked if we could make use of free gifts from surplus stock of magazines for children and teenagers. Soon after saying a puzzled: "Yes" - because the description of the objects we might be getting was so vague - we were presented with half-a-dozen large boxes full of exotic bric-a-brac. There were pens, pencils, crayons, rulers, miniature animal models (both natural and mythical!), bugs-with-parachutes, trolls, dolls, face glitter, bangles, badges, hair clips, scarves and many other items, some instantly recognisable and others not.

Clearly none had much intrinsic value, but our young pals Tom and Catherine who helped sort the miscellany viewed it in such an upbeat way that all the objects were obviously Very Desirable Things, at least so far as the younger generation was concerned. And if theirs was a typical response from young teenagers in our affluent country where many playthings now cost tens if not hundreds of pounds, then how much more likely were Hungarian kids to welcome them...? We were sure that this jolly junk would be really appreciated by church planters and leaders of children's work, where items could be given as prizes and the like, and help preserve slender church budgets in the process.

And that is how things turned out.

A typical response came from László and Erika, church planting in the Biblically historic town of Sárvár. The castle in this western

Hungarian town had hosted the first translation of the New Testament in that language in 1541, and its first printing in 1587.

More recently, Sárvár has been one of the hardest towns in the country to interest in the Christian message. László and Erika told us in mid-2001 that they had been church planting there for three years, but still saw only between one and six other people joining them for Sunday worship. As we will see later, the Lord is now beginning to reward their faithfulness, but when we gave them boxes of those free gifts they were still in need of all the encouragement anyone could muster.

Six months later Erika and László wrote: "We did not know what we could give for Christmas to the children and young people who had begun to attend our clubs... and your gifts were the perfect answers. We also found them very useful in the summer during the tent mission. Thank you again for helping meet the needs of our work in that way! Such things can make all the difference to the ways young people behave, and in their attitudes to us, and more importantly, the Gospel itself."

Getting things there

Many were the times we took to Hungary packs of those little gifts in our personal suitcases, at the expense of more or warmer clothing. Still other items travelled out on our Practical Team minibuses. We long felt restricted though, in what we could take or send, because weight and space have always been at a premium. For years we tried to find other means of transport - and generally failed. Trips like the one made by Gillian, David and Peter in 1996 with aid for Kőszeg have become prohibitively expensive now that meaningful competition between the Channel Tunnel and cross-channel ferries has faded into the past. We may conservatively reckon that to take even a small truck to Hungary today would cost a four-figure sum in basic costs alone.

Then, in the autumn of 2001 God began to answer our prayers for cheaper transport in an unexpected way. A friend of ours in the shoe manufacturing business encouraged Gillian and myself to contact Arthur, a dispatcher with an international freight company with a base at Avonmouth. This is the port of Bristol, and merely ten miles from home. Arthur, a Methodist, could not have been more helpful. Whenever possible, he said, he would put consignments of one or two units of 100 kilos each on their trucks to Budapest for a small Customs handling charge, or to Vienna for absolutely nothing!

In December 2001 we first took him at his word, sending 100 kilos of clothing, shoes, toys and children's writing materials to the group of Hungarian Baptist churches mentioned in passing in the previous chapter centred on Pacir in Vojvodina, northern Serbia. Remember, under the Milosevic regime in Yugoslavia this type of community had begun to be threatened by his policy of 'ethnic cleansing', and many members of it left voluntarily for Hungary, with the few personal possessions they were allowed to carry with them. The Hungarians who have remained in Vojvodina have not altogether recovered from the stresses of those nervous times, and still have fewer job and other opportunities than indigenous Serbs. Thus, any material help and personal encouragement we can give the Hungarian minority is worth much more than the 'market value' of any goods we may send. Other loads have gone to Ukraine.

More recently, the foot-and-mouth epidemic in the UK was to have unfortunate consequences for aid deliveries to that region. The disease was at least partly responsible for the Customs difficulties encountered on subsequent loads we sent to Budapest. In the end, persistence was always rewarded, but in October 2002 we tried a different strategy, and sent a large consignment to a depot near Vienna instead. Flying to Vienna Airport, it was a short journey for me in an estate car rented from the airport to pick everything up - and merely a ten-second wait for Customs clearance at the Austro-Hungarian border crossing at Hegyeshalom. That was so blissfully different from the three months of effort required to secure release of the previous load through Budapest! Vienna is likely to be the preferred route for the foreseeable future too. There is nothing illegal about our imports, but time is precious. Avoiding unnecessary form-filling and other delays is part of our Christian stewardship as we seek to maximise not only the use of the material resources entrusted to our care, but also the use of our every day and hour.

Anything to offer?

So, what of the future concerning 'aid' for the Hungarian world? This is firmly in the Lord's hands - and yours. In the past we have been offered some very unexpected things to pass on to some of His needy people. However, virtually everything we have been given has found its appointed place, and has been highly valued by our Hungarian friends. Remember, our loose change alone represents one or more days' pay for almost everyone we know out there. It is so encouraging for us to realise that God knows what we have and do not want, and can match it with what others need. There is no doubt that, in the days and years to come, we will all be cheered and sobered further as more of the things we would scarcely miss are passed on to people who will treasure them, and consider them truly blessings from the Lord. In His hands even the most mundane things - like toothbrushes - can and do unlock doors for the sharing of the Gospel and the strengthening of His Church by those who serve Him so unswervingly, while owning so few of the resources we take so much for granted.

CHAPTER 4

BUILDING FOR ETERNITY

New things to recognise in Recsk

It was five minutes to three. The first of the two thanksgiving services that weekend for the restoration work recently completed on the little chapel was about to begin. We had worked hard there eight weeks previously in September 2001, with our Seventh Practical Mission Team, alongside the pastor and the few able-bodied men from the Fellowship.

Suddenly an unwelcome thought crossed my mind: the main speaker had not yet appeared!

I nudged Erika, the pastor's wife, who was sitting next to me. "János isn't here!" I whispered. "What do you think we should do?"

She looked suitably startled. "I'll go and phone him on his mobile," she replied, and quickly and quietly slipped out of the packed hall.

A few minutes later, slightly flushed, she returned, with the Mission Secretary of the Hungarian Baptist Union close behind.

I breathed a sigh of relief, then settled down to enjoy the three-hour long celebration of God's goodness to His people in that out-of-the-way village. As recently as just a few months earlier His care for them in providing a much warmer, brighter and more comfortable place of worship had still not been expected by them - or us!

Afterwards, when the meeting had ended, the chief guests went to the pastor's house nearby for refreshments. I remarked to János that he had given us something of a fright: we had thought that he was not going to arrive on time. In the context of the previous few months his explanation became something I will always treasure.

"Well," he explained with a twinkle in his eye, "I had plenty of time really, but the church and its fence looked so different that I did not recognise it. So I drove straight past!"

Team membership

Since 1996 the number of church buildings and pastor's homes in Hungary where similar things could have happened because of the efforts of our Practical Teams has by now reached double figures. Involving over one hundred special friends from southern England and South Wales, the Teams have been loosely modelled on ones we earlier led to Billy-Montigny in the 1970s to help SGA missionary Bill Kapitaniuk establish his youth centre and base for operations eastward beyond the old Iron Curtain. The main purpose of our Hungarian Teams is similarly to help fellow Believers who have vision and energy for the Lord, but inadequate manpower or material resources to achieve by themselves the progress they wish to make with the repair or upgrading of their church-owned property. Our objective is always to see premises improved so that they are more fitting for use by the Lord's people, and more honouring to Him.

For every Team member it is a condition that he or she meets their own expenses, or raises them personally. Often this involves personal sacrifice - maybe the postponement of a planned holiday or something else for which they had been saving. In a few cases, friends who still cannot afford the full costs themselves are helped by others, even their home church fellowships. On one or two occasions we know that anonymous donors have stepped in to help also.

From the outset of this programme we have ensured that all the living costs of the Teams in Hungary are met by us, including the food we eat. Furthermore, gifts from prayer partners have always been forthcoming to ensure that there, 'on the field', we have been able to purchase all the necessary materials for our work.

Hungarians still generally find it difficult to make even their own ends meet. Thus, friends we go to help must not be put out of pocket themselves on account of expenses for anything they would not have bought if we had not gone to help THEM .

So what kinds of people have joined us in our Practical Mission Teams? Members of our Teams have come from the widest possible range of personal situations, married - travelling with or without their spouses - or single, engaged or widowed, working or retired, at school or college. They have ranged from professional scientists, architects, accountants and computer specialists through water bailiffs and farmers to builders, decorators, electricians, drivers and more besides. Housewives have valuably helped, plus students from schools, universities, and even police academies.

However, each and every member has been vital. These men, women and young persons have not only been prepared to sacrifice to join us, but once on site have also gladly worked hard, and slept in less (sometimes <u>much less</u>!) comfort than at home. They have also been prepared, if necessary, to drive or travel for up to 30 hours in each direction. Without them, the help we seek to provide to an increasing number of Hungarian churches simply would not be possible.

Because each Team is wholly made up of volunteers, we have to rely on the Lord to prompt the right mix of skills in every one. Even with the most careful planning in advance, it is not possible for the leaders to foresee every situation which might arise when the work is under way. Thus, it has always been a relief to leave Team selection to the Lord, the 'Master Builder' of His Church: the responsibility of the Team Leader is nothing more than to discover whom He wishes to employ! And in every single case we have found that we have had the right skills for the work in hand. There have been many times when, in the thick of the action some tricky task has presented itself, and someone has unexpectedly stepped forward to declare: "Ah, but <u>I know</u> how to do that!"

Sometimes the make up of a Team has been known to me weeks, or even months, in advance. On other occasions I have been left waiting until late, even <u>very</u> late, in the day for faith to be rewarded, like the time our 'Number One' driver pulled out on health grounds with only a week or so to go before the departure date. His replacement was found with merely two or three days to go.

Minuses and plusses

Predictably there have been many times when we have felt that our Teams, and we ourselves, have been under the attack of Satan. Will we ever forget the ten-hour delay to our overland party in northern France due to an engine failure? But, wonderfully, this happened just ten miles from a Ford Main Dealer, ensuring that recovery and repair costs were not too high. It was only later, though, that we realised these <u>exactly</u> totalled a sum which we were unexpectedly to save! Out of the blue away in Hungary, the locally owned minibus which took our air party to and from the airport at Ferihegy came to be provided for our benefit completely free of charge. We learned afterwards that at the last moment *Mátrametal*, the company that owned it, had been encouraged to view the two journeys as 'driver training'!

Nor shall we forget the night when Team member Jo fell ill, and had to be taken by paramedics to hospital in the nearby town of Eger with an acute attack of oesophagitis. We soon discovered the truth of the dictum in Hungary that it is easy to get <u>into</u> hospital, but it can be much more difficult to get <u>out again</u>! Two days later, when we were taking a service in a delightful little *imaház*, or prayer-house, in the village of Domoszló, 30 miles away, mobile phones began to ring. Both Jo - and husband Terry who, in a gesture foreign to our NHS, had been given a bed in a neighbouring ward so that he could be near his wife - desperately wished to rejoin the Team now Jo had recovered. Finishing my sermon, I went with a second driver and a Hungarian friend to act as interpreter to find the hospital, and hopefully release Jo while the rest of our Team had lunch at the prayer-house.

The chain of events that ensued seemed to owe more to James Bond movies than Christian missionary activity. First we had to gain access to the hospital. Once this, with some difficulty, had been achieved we then had to locate the correct ward. Getting there afforded us some interesting glimpses of more venerable parts of the hospital, as well as the newer ones where Jo and Terry were concerned. At last we found them - but then needed someone to agree that she could be discharged. At first we were told that this was not possible on a Sunday, but persistence led us to a charming lady doctor who, in the end, relented and agreed that Jo could go. She insisted, though, that I would be responsible for Jo's condition thereafter... but then posed smilingly with us all for souvenir photographs. You can imagine how glad I was at the end of the week when Jo finished it in good health.

Meanwhile, later that same Sunday afternoon I was relieved to be able to get the minibus back to the *imaház* in time to pick up the rest of the Team, and move on to our next engagement. This was with SGA-supported church planters Jonatón and Örsi in Gyöngyös. We timed our arrival to the minute!

Then there is an episode I recall from an earlier Team mission. Tracey, abroad for the very first time and therefore new to the rigours of a Practical Mission, will never forget that it was her suitcase which should be the one not to appear on the baggage claim conveyor belt in Vienna. Of all the hundreds of cases our Team members have taken, hers had to be the first to go astray. It was some days before Tracey and her case were reunited. But, despite the problems this caused, she was glad to confirm recently: "I learned a lot about myself that week," and confirmed again how pleased she was that she had been a member of the Team.

Some other potentially sticky moments have even had amusing aftermaths. On one Practical Mission there had been niggling problems with the elderly English minibus which had been on duty as our ground support vehicle. On the return trip to England with the overland contingent of our party, its engine cut out whilst driving up the ramp at Dover's Hoverport. There was only one way to shift the van - by all the passengers getting out to push! As they did so, An up-market new saloon edged by. Its driver pointed to the church address on the side of the stricken minibus, and sneered: "You should try praying!"

A few minutes later the engine of the minibus was successfully jump-started. A few minutes later still, some way away from the docks, the Team found the traffic forming two lanes. In the right hand one, which they took, it was moving steadily. The left hand one, though, soon came to a standstill. The Team saw they were gaining rapidly on the large car, for it was trapped among the stationary traffic.

Mike could not resist an opportunity this presented for witness. Quickly winding down the driver's window as they swept past, he leant out and cried with more than a pinch of pleasure: "We do pray, mate, EVERY DAY!"

And, speaking of pleasure, virtually everyone who has been on a Practical Mission has returned home on a 'spiritual high', tired but grateful to God for so many personal blessings while serving Him in Hungary. Indeed, most praise Him long before they return. Another Mike, one of our builders, but at the time quite a new Christian, looked tired towards the end of the inaugural working day on the very first of the Practical Missions.

"How's it going, Mike? I ventured tentatively.

I shall never forget the slow, beaming smile that spread across his face as he replied: "Fine, thank you, Eric. I've not enjoyed a day's work so much in my whole life!"

The reason for this was, of course, that Mike had not worked before with a gang wholly made up of fellow Christians. Indeed, few of us do normally, because of the ways we have to make our livings in a dominantly non-Christian world. Maybe it was because of the personal benefits Team members reap that a British mission leader once remarked to me concerning the Practical Missions: "You are ministering to folks in the UK!" - implying that we were helping our Team members more than we were helping our friends in Hungary.

My reply was swift: "Well, if God does bless our Teams, I'm really glad. But THE CONCRETE IS OUT THERE...!"

Happily, more and more Brothers and Sisters in the Lord in central and eastern Europe are overjoyed that we can be a help and blessing to them, even if it can cost us quite a lot to achieve that goal.

The Pápa picture

Speaking of concrete, this first featured in the programme of the very first Practical Mission to Hungary in 1996. Most of that concrete was in the north west of the country at Josef and Wendy's new base in Pápa, a town named after the Pope. Our work there was connected with the new church Wendy and Josef had recently been called to plant.

"Two Christian girls have pressed us to plant a new evangelical church in Pápa," Josef had explained to us soon after we met him in 1965. "Wendy and I believe we should try to do this, and are moving there very shortly. We want to begin by meeting in the ground floor room of the semi-detached house we will rent near the bus station. We will need to make quite a lot of changes to the building, though. Could you bring some friends to help?"

In the fast changing modern world the Lord calls many of us to serve Him in different ways and in different places at different times in our lives. Gillian and I remembered the year of our engagement and those early years of our marriage when we had several times taken teams to help in Billy-Montigny, northern France. We also recognised that my 16 years of radio ministry to the old USSR and elsewhere had recently come to a happy end, as explained in Chapter 6. Therefore Gillian and I were sure that Josef's invitation was a new challenge we might to accept. Through our earlier trips to northern France we had learnt a lot about the organisation of Christian working parties, and now felt ready to venture much further afield with such a group.

Also, since the times we had helped Bill and Sophie Kapitaniuk in the late 1960s and early 1970s, I myself had often arranged and led student field classes as part of my responsibilities in the University of Bristol's School of Geographical Sciences. Organising further Christian 'field trips' would be somewhat similar, though a much greater pleasure!

Last but not least, from the 1980s I had become responsible for organising and hosting international scientific conferences which had required planning down to the very finest detail. I recall once being on the phone when an academic visitor came to my University of Bristol office. What clearly impressed him most was not the NASA-funded research I was doing then. Rather, it was the fact that my phone call was to purchase plastic spoons for the coffee and tea breaks at a related conference for which I was responsible.

"If necessary," he appositely enthused, "a good leader must be prepared to do <u>anything</u> himself!"

On the other hand, of course, family and friends know that, when it comes to actually doing things practical (maybe a few aspects of interior decorating apart) I am a total novice. There have been occasions when expert Team members have thought it necessary even to show me the correct way to hold a hammer! However, when the Apostle Paul wrote about Christian gifting he emphasised that different gifts are entrusted to different people.

Like carpentry or plumbing. Practical Team leadership is just one of those gifts. And though this should not be thought of as the most important, at least it is probably the most demanding in terms of time, for it includes both pre-event planning - which usually begins some six months before each mission - and many post-event activities, plus all sorts of things in between. Thus in 1996, saying: "Yes!" to Josef and Wendy was the easy part. Through the past few years the work of organising the seven practical missions to the time of writing - then the eighth, planned for Nyírbátor in September 2003 - has been a considerable and ongoing task. But it also quickly became one Gillian and I enjoyed, and on which we worked together well as our own mini management team.

The Pápa mission itself was to prove both a blessing and a great success. Some of our First Practical Mission Team of 15 cleaned, filled, painted and top-coated the walls, ceiling and woodwork of the main living room in Josef and Wendy's new home so that this could serve as the meeting place for their embryonic church. Meanwhile, others laid a concrete drive outside, carpentered side gates, repaired damaged doors and window frames, and even artistically relaid the front garden. Josef was specially thrilled with the newly fitted shelving in his little study, housing his modest personal computer and rows of theological books: "Now I can prepare some proper sermons again!" he enthused.

So, towards the end of that week we were all tired but thrilled to be able to participate in the first service ever held in that building. We were accompanied, of course, by Nóra and Emeké. These are the two young ladies who had so long prayed that an evangelical church might be planted in their town. The simple, uncomplicated yet very moving celebration of the Lord's Supper that followed the time of worship and testimony seemed specially in keeping with the simple surroundings.

Immediately God began to bless that tiny new family of His people. Indeed, just three years later we were invited back to Pápa with another Team. This was already our Fifth, because in one hectic year we had taken not one Team to Hungary but two, one in spring and one in autumn. Why Pápa again? Because by then the original Baptist Mission had so outgrown its original home that it urgently needed fresh and larger premises, in which the Fellowship could be properly constituted as a church.

In April 1999 Josef and Wendy showed us a recently closed restaurant some 30 yards along the street from the rambling old town house that English friends had recently and unexpectedly bought for them. With its dingy décor, out-of-date facilities and derelict courtyard, those premises would require a thorough overhaul to make them at all suitable for prayer and worship. The only parts which seemed 'smart' enough and in sufficiently good repair were the small side rooms which had obviously been used as a brothel. However, in the spirit of Michaelangelo, who is reported to have remarked of a highly-undesirable looking block of marble: "I see an ANGEL in it!", so Wendy brightly said of that unsavoury area: "This will make a perfect Sunday School area. It even has its own wash room for the children."

The biggest challenge for our team, though, was certain to be Josef's wish to cover the inner courtyard. This was full of junk and rubble, and completely open to all weathers. "We would like to put a canopy over that," he explained, "so that it can be a kind of lobby, and so the children and their teachers don't get wet or cold as they go from the church to their Sunday School classroom and back."

A few weeks later, a Hungarian architect's plans for such a canopy plopped through our letterbox. We showed these to a new English friend who had recently introduced himself to us after a meeting in a church in Wiltshire where we had talked about our Practical Teams. "I know someone who would like to come on your next Practical Mission," he had quietly said.

On asking enquiringly who that might be, he had shyly admitted: "ME"!

Since then, as an architect Tim has figured very importantly in all our more recent Practical Missions. Indeed he has also sometimes travelled out with us on our reconnaissance trips, and on a couple of other occasions has gone out alone at the request of Hungarian churches to give his expert advice and help on other projects.

Looking at his Hungarian counterpart's concept drawings for a curved, free-standing canopy in Pápa, he responded quite negatively. He did not think that scheme would work. Subsequent enquiries proved him right. For one thing, the curved perspex required for that plan is virtually unobtainable in Hungary, and would be very expensive to purchase in the UK, even if it were then possible to transport it to that country.

Tim further averred that a canopy fixed to the neighbouring walls would have a number of major advantages over the original free standing one. He promised to become a member of our team in September, and would help design and supervise the erection of a canopy that would be more practical to build, and made of materials which would be both available and affordable in Hungary. In consultation with our carpenter Howard, and Josef in Pápa, new and practicable plans were drawn up.

That September we urgently needed dry weather both for the work in Pápa and for a parallel project in nearby Győr which involved a detachment of men from our Fifth Practical Mission Team. The Lord wonderfully obliged. The weather was warm and sunny the whole of that week. So, by the very last afternoon of our stay the interior of the old restaurant dining room in Pápa had already become eminently worthy of use as a worship space. Indeed, the dozen or so of us in the Team had already joined together in it with over 20 local friends the previous Sunday for a morning service. That congregation again included Nóra and Emeké, who were particularly delighted by that first-ever meeting of God's people in the newly christened 'Cornerstone Church'. True, even when the time came for us to leave for home the former band platform, from which slender Emeké had been laboriously digging out a baptistry, had still to be completed. But the splendid courtyard canopy had come together with a final rush, and was finished with maybe two hours to spare. This has since been the most admired feature of the new church complex.

Today it is hard to remember that the same canopy had also presented Tim, Howard and others with the stiffest of technical tests. "This is the most difficult thing I have ever been asked to do," Tim had ruefully remarked at one point.

How he and Howard, with help from John, David and other men ever managed to fit their convincingly regular-looking geometrical creation, with its crisp, triangular profile into a space bounded by irregular building lines, bowed walls, and wavy roofs has always mystified me. But fit it in they did, and their creation has brought the other elements of those old structures together in a most effective and visually pleasing way.

Today the young church continues to be blessed, and is already nearly full for family services, when more than 50 folk meet for worship and to enjoy 'The Word'. Many new Believers have been added to the Church of Jesus Christ in Pápa, having met Him first in the Cornerstone Church premises. Several have since been baptised in the green-and-white tiled tank whose space Emeké had worked so hard in high temperatures to excavate. But we should not be surprised by all this, for when the Lord's people are true to their calling, are fully committed to Him, and make conscious efforts to honour Him in everything, He will surely bless.

Győr jaunts

Thinking back a little further again, the very first church Gillian and I had visited in the mid-1990s after my long absence from Hungary was the Baptist church in Győr, the important industrial city of over 100,000 inhabitants in the north-west corner of the country. However, at that time even to find the church was a considerable challenge. To do so one had to enter the gateway to an ordinary, middle-aged apartment block opposite the city centre park, go into the building itself, then along a corridor, out the back, in through a side entrance, up some stairs and finally into the enlarged room used for worship. Even this was not very large, and was full whenever about 40 people crowded in.

Most strikingly though, it was clear that a more private place would have been hard to envisage. In the 'Old Days', its secret nature had been a blessing, for the congregation had been able to meet without drawing much attention to itself. However, in the sudden freedom of the new era, to be so hidden was no longer an advantage, and the room had already become too small to accommodate everyone who wanted to attend. Moreover, it was scarcely satisfactory that the bedroom was the only possible venue the apartment afforded for the new Sunday School, and the kitchen had to double as the vestry.

János and Csilla, the young pastor and his wife, along with other leaders of the church, became sure a move to bigger premises was vital. But it took great faith as well as vision when the Lord clearly pointed them to the former Red Star Cinema as the best answer to their need. Now empty, this was merely 200 yards away, though much more prominent and well-known, being very near Győr's ornate, impressive City Hall. No longer a venue for communist propaganda films, the Red Star was available for purchase. It was also larger - MUCH larger - than the 'church in the flats'. The main auditorium alone had been designed to seat over 300 in space and comfort!

Echoing the Apostle Paul, János remarked at the time that: *"It seemed good to the Holy Spirit and to us"* (Acts 15:28) to make a bid for the empty cinema, and so the church leaders had done so. There was a hill of opposition to climb on the city council - but much more significantly from the standpoint of the Fellowship, a mountain of a price to scale. However, in great faith the church committed itself to find the purchase sum over the next three years. In partial answer to the prayers of the members, both gifts and interest-free loans were soon forthcoming from the UK, but much sacrificial living and giving were soon in evidence among the small membership itself.

Gillian and I caught one highly challenging glimpse of such activity one or two years later. While paying a brief Practical Mission planning visit to Győr we stayed with one of the older couples from the church in their humble little home. Returning quite late one evening we found Mikhail and Irénka meticulously labouring away at the table in their kitchen-cum-dining-cum-reception room. Boxes of tiny gadgets seemed to be everywhere.

"What are you doing?" we enquired. The answer was to tax not only our limited knowledge of Hungarian, but our dictionary too.

"We're assembling the control systems for Audi car windscreen wiper blades," was what we finally understood them to say.

"But however many are you making?" I queried with eyebrows raised, reflecting on the rank upon rank of containers and miniscule spare parts strewn across the table top.

Mikhail smiled, then wrote two figures in the margin of an old newspaper: "1 year, 100,000".

Gillian and I gasped in unison.

At first: "So many?" was all I could think to say, once I had found my voice. "But WHY?"

"To help pay for our new church building," came the matter-of-fact reply.

I did some quick mental arithmetic. If dear Mikhail and Irénka shared that task equally it would mean either of them completing nearly 200 control sets every single night of the year, excepting

Sundays. I glanced round the frugally furnished little cottage room. That dear couple had so few of this world's goods... but both were clearly amassing troves of treasure in Heaven!

And there is a sequel to this sobering story of costly devotion to the purposes of God. At home a year or so later, when glancing through a recent copy of *Motoring Which*, I chanced upon some tables listing the good and bad points of a wide range of modern car models. Somewhat curiously I looked down the lists until I found the Audi section, then scanned across for the appraisal of the windscreen wipers of the types with which I knew Mikhail and Irénka were concerned. It emerged that they were among the most highly rated features of those particular models - and more highly so than the windscreen wiper systems on most other makes of cars. Yes, our two friends in Györ had been toiling away so intently on those tiny items to help raise funds for the purchase of the former cinema. But even in their eagerness to finish as many as possible they had not forgotten that this was a: *"...labour in the Lord"* (1 Corinthians 15:58). For them, quality and quantity had to go hand in hand.

And how we later rejoiced to see God meeting all the financial needs of His people in the newly consecrated church! We revisited Györ three months prior to date by which the third and final payment on the former cinema was due. The money in hand was way short of what was required: "Please pray that the Lord will do a miracle in this situation," János and others had pleaded.

We heard later that God had indeed answered the prayers that they, and we, and many others prayed... and had done so with just THREE DAYS to spare!

Of course, much effort was needed also to clean the old picture-house to fit it for its new and very different function. Towards the end of the week we spent in Pápa with our First Practical Mission Team in 1996, a down payment was made on the building, in return for the keys for the old cinema from the City Council. So it was our happy lot to be able to help with some of the initial cleaning and repainting of the main doors and vestibule, in readiness for an opening act of worship on the Sunday before the commencement of our homeward journey that same afternoon. Our 15 pairs of hands more than doubled those available from the members of the local Fellowship. The tasks confronting us were vast, and often far from savoury. For example, it fell to another Tim to remove dead pigeons from one room open to the sky, and help clean long-neglected loos.

Meanwhile, Gillian spent hours one day on her knees in the auditorium, chipping up black globs of congealed chewing gum from the floor. These had been cast under foot by generations of film-goers, and pressed hard into the red and tan linoleum by their feet. The sight of Gillian emerging from one such session with blackened patches on her trousers, and so stiff that she could scarcely stand upright, is one indelible memory from that time - though even more memorable is the happy smile she wore...!

So, on the Sunday morning at the end of the First Practical Mission we were able to enjoy that inaugural meeting in the new 'Morning Star Christian Ministry Centre' - as Győr Baptist Church is now known. The meeting had to be held in the foyer, for this was the only part of the building to have been cleaned sufficiently after merely two days of effort. However, even this former ticket office was bigger than the old church room in the flats. The event itself was the once-monthly service of the English Church in Győr. For us this became another truly historic and joyful occasion, and a most appropriate one with which to end a truly memorable week.

The very next autumn our Second Practical Team came to be based in Győr itself, to give further much-needed help with the redecoration of other large parts of the new church premises. Most of these were still wearing the pale green, powdery, lime-based paint applied when it had been built more than 40 years previously. Among our tasks were to help clean and decorate a room to serve as a caretaker's bedsit, and to do the same for one of the former projection rooms now to be used by the Sunday School. It came as a big surprise to Pastor János and myself when the lightly tinted off-white paints we had chosen for the latter room emerged from the cans as mid-intensity pink and blue. But Csilla at least was very pleased: "What lovely WARM COLOURS for the children!" she enthused unprompted, so we were happy too.

Others of that Team also helped treat scores of moulded plastic stacking chairs sent from a church in England. These were urgently needed by the Morning Star for its growing congregations. Unfortunately the chairs had clearly spent some time in the open air before they had been shipped out, so the legs had to have much rust removed before they could be repainted. Meanwhile, still others of our group repaired electrics, and installed new switches and light fittings in several parts of the building.

Another year on we took a Third Team to that same corner of Hungary, though in that case to help simultaneously not in one or two locations, but in four! Suffice it to say for the moment that we left a small detachment in Győr to install a rather vital water supply to the church kitchen, and a shower near the pastor's office and the caretaker's flat. How everyone concerned had previously managed without direct water supplies in those parts of the building remains a mystery to me.

A year later again, in September 1999, most of our Fifth Practical Mission Team helped establish the Cornerstone Church in Pápa, including the erection of that much-admired canopy described earlier in this chapter. Four brave men from our Team were assigned to Győr to help with the hazardous task of re-rendering the exterior of the Morning Star's very sizeable shell. Being a big job, helpers had been enlisted from Baptist churches as far afield as Pécs and Szeged, literally at the other end of the country. As in Nehemiah's day: *"...the people worked with all their heart"* (Nehemiah 4:6) so that the result would be more honouring to Him. How exciting it was to observe, high on the redecorated front façade, its new cross lit at night, and lifted up for all in the city centre to see. We were delighted too that a local firm of Christian decorators were repainting the entire interior of the auditorium free of charge, for there had been no budget for this.

Meanwhile, the scaffholding on the exterior, so wonky and unsafe to Western eyes, had been loaned without charge by the city's Public Works Department. This was because the mayor had come to recognise how much good the church was doing in the community. For one thing, he knew about the washkits from the UK which members had delivered to the Mother-and-Baby Unit as described in the previous chapter. For another, as will be explained in Chapter 8, the Deputy Mayor had recently enjoyed a private concert in the Council Chamber in the City Hall, given by a famous Welsh Christian choir which we had arranged to visit Győr as part of its annual International Music Festival.

All this reminded me of the very last message that had been delivered in the 'house church' room in the apartment block three years earlier, on the very evening of the unforgettable first service in the Morning Star. Although the rest of our Team at that time had already left for home, Gillian and I were staying behind as planned for a day or two longer, and were struck by the theme of Josef's final address in the church's old, cramped, premises.

"Until now," Josef thought-provokingly pointed out to the congregation, "you have been a '<u>private</u>' church... but you are about to become a very <u>public</u> one! Few other people even knew there was a church here at all, but everyone in the city will soon know there is one in the old cinema. Are you personally prepared for the changes that will bring? Maybe not many of your friends know you are a Christian. Very soon everyone will know us all as followers of Jesus Christ. There will be great new opportunities in this - and there may also be extra <u>personal cost</u>! But remember that Jesus exercised His ministry very publicly, and He wants us to do the same. *'Let your light shine before men,'* He said in Matthew 5, *'that they may see your good deeds, and praise your Father in Heaven.'* "

As Josef was speaking there was some pensiveness, perhaps even apprehension, on the faces of many in the audience as they faced the fact that church life was never going to be the same for them again.... Yes, they got Josef's message! And time has proved both that Josef was right, and that the Morning Star Fellowship has been given the grace to match the fresh and greater challenges that have been presented by the move to its new spiritual home.

Gillian and I wondered two things as we left for England. The first was this: "How many years will it take for that small church family to fill its huge new church?" The second was "Would we ourselves ever see it filled?"

The astonishing answer to question one was to prove to be: "Merely THREE MONTHS!" for, in December 1996, we heard that the 300-seater auditorium was full for a special Christmas service. Chairs had to be borrowed from nearby public buildings to seat many of those who came, for this was before we had helped refresh the load of chairs which had come from England, and the church did not have enough of its own. And in answer to the second question, we ourselves were to see the Morning Star completely filled in the middle of 1998 for the visit of *Cambrensis*, the celebrated Christian choir from South Wales whose special concert tour will be described more fully later in the book.

Kőszeg clips

So far in this chapter we have talked about earlier Practical Missions aimed at helping establish new homes for whole church families, large or small. The emphasis of the middle missions came to be somewhat different, mainly focussing on improved living accommodation for key Christian families.

As mentioned earlier, concrete featured prominently in the First Practical Mission in Pápa. It did so too in Kőszeg where, way back during the First Practical Mission, three of our fittest men were despatched for an exhausting 48 hours. Their task was to help Pastor Attila, his wife Erzsébét and their family by laying a concrete drive to their new but unfinished house. Donát, the fourth child of that dear couple, suffered oxygen starvation at birth and is severely spastic. It was already obvious in 1996 that it would be a long time - if ever - before he would be able to walk by himself. A firm surface instead of the muddy path to their front door would be such a help to his family, not least his slightly built Mum. She would find it so much easier to wheel Donát in a pushchair rather than having to carry him from the lane to their doorstep.

Attila, like most Hungarian pastors was building the new family home himself. Many Hungarian people still do this today. The downstairs part of their house is reasonably complete, but upstairs has still not been finished to this day. When we first visited in 1996 it had not even been begun. From the early 1990s, though, the church Attila pastors has met in his home, doing so three or four times each week. Because the kitchen, dining area and living room are one continuous open space, and the two teenage daughters, Ággie and Klára also slept there, they could never think of going to bed until every visitor had left. To help them, we felt constrained to create at least one of the new rooms planned for the first floor level, upstairs within the A-shaped roof.

So, while the plumbing party of our Third Practical Mission Team worked in Győr, another half set about battening, insulating and plaster boarding the upstairs space in that needy home in Kőszeg. New stud walls were necessary too, and here we ran into a snag.

In the UK whenever more sawn timber is required, it is a simple matter to pop along to a do-it-yourself store and pick up what is required. In Hungary that was, and largely still is impossible today. Some timber had been ordered in advance for the wall frames, but the unexpected need for a dropped ceiling had consumed more than had been planned. So the wood in hand soon ran out. Recourse had to be made to metal frames for the main stud walls which divided the new room from the rest of the space under the roof. Precious time was lost in the process of obtaining the new materials, and working out how to use the patented metal system. Later in the week reinforcements arrived in the shape of the plumbing group from Győr, plus three more of the Team who had been helping in another pastor's home in the town of Sárvár 30 miles away. However, to our dismay we were unable to make up all the time which had been lost, and we had to leave with the job as a whole only about three-quarters done.

Unhappy that we had not been able to achieve our goal, Gillian and I organised an additional, smaller-than-usual Fourth Practical Mission Team of seven during the next spring of 1999, to return and complete the job. With a smaller Team, the ground support vehicle travelling out from England could be smaller too, and faster than usual. We were overjoyed when friends from our church lent us their Toyota Previa people-carrier for that purpose. Quick and comfortable, this was ideal for the four men who went overland, plus the toolbags which, as usual went that way also. Toolkits usually weigh too much to go out by air. The 'overlanders' were to make Hungary in record time - at speeds unmatched by any of our teams before or since.

On that occasion the work went well, and it proved possible not only to finish the big new room, but adjacent wash rooms too. So as to prevent heat loss up the now open stair well, we left a modest sum for a local builder to box off the big gaps remaining open to the rest of the uninsulated roof space. At last Ággie and Klára would be able to enjoy the privacy teenagers so covet: disappearing to do their homework, relax, or whatever else they chose, and when they chose to do so, without having to wait for the last guests to leave the house.

So the family was delighted... and we were too, though just before we left for home Pastor Attila gave me acute cause for thought. Indicating he had a question on his mind, in his quiet way he enquired: "What do you want us to do with the new room?"

I was absolutely stunned. Here was a dear man of God, who had earlier been persecuted by the communists, and who now worked long hours at a dirty job he disliked intensely so that he could lead the local Baptist congregation. His whole family serves the Lord unceasingly, extra burdened as it is by Donát's special needs. And this Hungarian Christian hero was actually asking me how he should USE HIS OWN HOME...?

Knowing it would be more convenient for all, and less disruptive for the family if the church continued to meet downstairs, I stressed that we had created the new room: "For the family only to use," and he seemed pleased with this. But we drove away more conscious than usual of all the private space, comforts and possessions we have in our own land, yet which we so often take for granted.

But I remain sad to this day that we have, thus far, been unable to arrange for a handyman or two to spend just a few days in Kőszeg to make the bare, irregular, handrail-less staircase from the living room safer, and much smarter too....

Sárvár service

Meanwhile, what of that small group from our Third Team who had been in Sárvár during the busy September of 1998? László and Erika had moved to that historic town the year before to begin church planting. Their apartment is above a shop not far from Sárvár Castle. As we saw in Chapter 3 it was there in the Sixteenth Century that part of the Scriptures had been translated into Hungarian and printed in that language for the first time.

Sadly, in Sárvár more than four hundred years later there is virtually nothing to show for that remarkable piece of Hungarian Christian history. True, there are a couple of venerable church buildings in the town, but no evangelical witness and maybe no more than a handful of Bible-believing Christians in the whole district. Once the scene of wonderful pioneering work for the Lord, Sárvár is now one of the toughest places in the whole of Hungary for sharing the Gospel. László and Erika have since found this out.

On our very first visit to László and Erika's flat we found it to be an interesting one, with sloping ceilings and dormer windows. Though quite new when they moved in, like Attila and Erzsébét's house it was as yet unfinished. Electric wires sprouted like proverbial spaghetti from one junction box, walls had not been top coated with paint, and the floor in the largest room was still bare concrete. It was not a safe environment for two small boys, let alone an attractive one for prayer meetings, counselling and other informal church-planting activities. It was clear that without the kind of help we could provide, and the materials we could afford to buy, nothing would be done to improve it for months or even years ahead.

So we despatched Karl to attend to the electrics, Jim to supervise the laying of a polished timber tongue-and-groove floor, painter Tim to decorate the walls and Karl's wife, Helen to lend another pair of hands wherever they were needed most. In merely three days a quite elegant room emerged from the rough space that had been there before.

"We thought we would have to close the door to that room for ages," László said when all was finished. "This is <u>such a big encouragement and blessing</u> to us, for we can begin using it right away!"

And so they did, and have done so to the present day. This is where their shelves of Christian books and tapes for borrowing by enquirers have been housed, and where much prayer has been offered up to God, not least during the next few difficult and frustrating years. In the summer of 2001 László and Erika recounted to us in that very room the sobering fact that, after three years of dedicated effort, still only between one and six other friends would meet with them in the local school room for Sunday afternoon services.

Imagine how very glad I was to hear on a subsequent visit in the autumn of 2002 that the Lord was at last beginning to more fulsomely reward their labours. Numbers on Sunday were increasing. Around 15 children were now coming to their week night kid's club, with twice as many for special events, and a dozen or so teenagers were attending their own Friday evening meetings. Both these types of gatherings were taking place in that room with the lovely shiny floor our Team members had laid. Best of all, László and Erika told of the first baptismal service they had recently arranged for new convert Judit. A second such celebration of the saving power of Jesus Christ was already being planned for the month that followed....

Komárom challenges

Last but not least in respect of the Practical Team 'home help trilogy' begun in Kőszeg and Sárvár, mention must be made of the input we were able to make in Komárom on the south bank of the Danube where today it faces Slovakia on the other shore. Komárom was where most of the work of our Sixth Practical Mission Team was undertaken in the autumn of the year 2000. Here we helped Pastor Zsolt and other willing hands from the little Baptist church to redecorate the whole of its dignified exterior, and to renovate the adjoining run-down apartment. This is the apartment now lived in by Gábor and Joli, of whom we knew nothing at the time, but of whom we will say more in Chapter 5. Thus, in September 2002 we were also oblivious of the important part Komárom would soon play in the chain of events the Lord had planned to serve His purposes in other entirely different ministry directions.

Over 100 years old, the church complex in Komárom has thick outer walls of stone, but we soon found that some inner walls were made of bricks of mud and straw. These quickly crumbled, even at the merest tap of a hammer. Worse still, while running our initial checks with architect Tim, we discovered that the floorboards had been lain straight onto a clinker base, and the window lintels were nothing but bundles of reeds. Finally, having no proper damp courses, the inner surfaces of the outer walls were crumbling and their plaster flaking off.

When September came our builders were much exercised by the implications of these and other interesting little challenges. Meanwhile, our painting gang under the leadership of John had real fun mixing lime wash for the outside walls, and the decorative 'headlines' which adorned them. In the apartment, ripping out old windows and their frames, and replacing them with new lintels and modern double-glazed window units proved stiff physical challenges. So too was the task of laying the top layer of screed on the fresh concrete floors which men of the church had put down before our arrival on the site.

My own main task - management and devotional leadership apart - was frequent shopping with part-time evangelist Sándor. We had to obtain all the materials as and when required, plus fittings for the new kitchen designed to replace the existing corner of an outhouse which had previously been used for such a purpose, as well as the upgraded toilet facilities and shower. There were also two new gas fires to buy for the two rooms we were creating out of an original one, so as to separate a reception area from a bedroom. Working alongside Sándor, Józsi, István, Pastor Zsolt and others from the Komárom Fellowship, the week flew by but everyone was delighted with the progress that was made.

Special memories of that wonderful Sixth Mission include the truly tasty meals, even though these were delivered from local school kitchens. Eaten in the church garden, and costing no more than 60p each per head, they compared well with many restaurant meals back home. A drinks service was maintained by lovely ladies of the church, especially Sándor's wife Ággie, and István's Slovakian wife, Hedvige. Then there was the evening barbecue when, along with several families from the church, we burnt a great bonfire of bits and pieces left over from the construction work, and praised God together with musical accompaniment by Tony and David on their guitars, and Terry on one or other of his bagful of mouth organs.

How we praised God for the beautiful weather He gave us all that week too. It had been drizzling the evening we arrived, but no further rain fell until a few large drops landed on the windscreens of our two rental cars nearing the Austro-Hungarian border as they ferried the air party to Vienna Airport at the very end of the Mission.

Being very busy as team leader, I am always aware that things happen of which I hear nothing until later. Apparently in Komárom some of the men got into the habit of taking early morning walks from the very basic but convenient motel where we were staying, down to the Danube maybe half a mile away. On the last evening Gillian and I discovered that such a trek meant twice crossing the main railway lines from Vienna to Budapest, here some six tracks wide and on a fast stretch of the line. Sometimes it required a quick dash across the tracks as trains were heard in the distance… and apparently more than one of our men had been keen to get extra good, close up action shots of passing expresses…!

Fortunately all lived to tell the tale, and Gillian and I returned to Komárom for a short visit the following spring. This was not only to: *"Bring a massage in the morning service,"* as Pastor Zsolt's slightly incorrect English email had charmingly asked me to do, but also to see what progress had been made with finding the new youth workers by whom the renovated apartment was intended to be used. It was then we first met Gábor and Joli. As the next chapter will relate, they were to be crucial links with another type of entirely new project of which we ourselves at that time were still completely ignorant.

But of the Sixth Mission itself, perhaps the most abiding memory is how hard all the men from that small church worked too, whether on 'holiday', or after a long day's normal work was done. In particular, who could forget the efforts of those officially 'retired'? Most memorable of them was Józsi's 94-year old Dad. Well under five feet tall, his slight frame would always have been unsuited to heavy jobs, but all he could do he did. This included the thankless task of sorting out the pebbles from the mixed load of sand and gravel that had been obtained to constitute more of the concrete we have left in Hungary.

But no, Józsi Senior's work was no more 'thankless' than our own, for does not God say in His Word that all: *"Those who honour Me I will honour..."* (1 Samuel 2:30)?

Bicske and Recsk reminiscences

To complete the building stories to the time of writing, we may recall the old wedding rhyme: *"Something old and something new, something borrowed and something blue."*

It was just as well that our Sixth Team to Komárom had been a large one for shortly before our departure from England I had had a pressing email from Pastor Lajos in Bicske. It said this: "We hope you will be able to bring a team to help us here, and stay for several months!"

In 1998, Lajos and his wife Mariann had begun church planting in that sleepy market town some 30 miles west of Budapest. Easily accessed by the Hungarian M1 motorway which closely bypasses the town on its northern side, Bicske is now facing the prospect of becoming a dormitory for the capital. In the spring of 2000 we had been shown a site near the motorway which had once been a transport depot, and to which the Lord seemed to be pointing the youthful but quickly growing Fellowship as a possible location for their first permanent church premises. The long, low prefabricated former office block seemed a reasonable place into which to move. At least it was much bigger than the rented café they had been using near the bus station!

Although our planning for the mission that September had been largely complete for some time, we were glad to be able to detach half-a-dozen pairs of hands from the work in Komárom on four separate days to help with the initial cleaning and modification of the prefab in Bicske. Expert advice was, as usual, forthcoming from architect Tim. I shall always remember how his eyes lit up as we initially rounded the corner and he first saw the prefab: "Many years ago," he quietly explained, "I attended a course on that type of structure. From that day to this, I did not know WHY I had to do so - BUT NOW I DO!"

With Tim's informed inputs, Alan, David, Mike and others moved inner partitions to reshape some of the rooms, while Gillian and Sue repainted window frames. Abby, Andrew, Peter and I cleaned and colour rollered walls and ceilings in a range of new, fresh shades, aided by Béla, Tibi, and Tamás.

Come Sunday the first worship service in that building was a joyful time indeed, though it was already clear from the size of the congregation that a larger worship area than the one we had helped prepare would soon be necessary. But Tim had taken pains to explain to Lajos that, because of the rigid nature of the structure, it would not be possible to move any more of its inside walls without threatening the whole with collapse when the wind blew strongly!

Using one rim of the borrowed, portable baptismal tank as a makeshift desk, Tim later suggested some possible ways an extra building could look on adjacent open ground. Excitingly, in September 2002 the foundations for such a new structure were begun with the help of men from a church in Clevedon, North Somerset - but that aspect is more properly the subject of Chapter 8.

Rather, recalling once again the old, jingly wedding couplet, if Bicske Baptist Church was therefore the scene of: *"Something borrowed"* and of: *"something new"*, then the village of Recsk up in the Mátra Mountains was soon to witness: *"something old,"* becoming: *"something blue"*. As usual Gillian and I paid springtime visits in 2001 to a short list of possible venues for our next Practical Mission, all suggested to us by leaders of the Hungarian Baptist Union. We were soon to feel embarrassed, though, for as soon as we set foot in the first of them we had an electric feeling that: "THIS IS IT!"

Amazingly, very shortly after the terror camp described in Chapter 1 had been established on the quarried hillside overlooking Recsk, the then already 50-year old synagogue in the village in the valley had passed into the care of a little group of brave Baptists. Previously they had been meeting in a private house. Despite all the excesses of the current communist regime, and the awful shadow the camp cast over the whole community, these Believers were determined to be as public as they could be in their church life and witness for the Lord Jesus Christ. On its plot opposite the mayor's offices, the converted synagogue could easily be kept under close scrutiny, but God honoured His people, and kept them safe. Maybe embarrassed by the terrible tales filtering down from the mountain, the Communist Party in Recsk itself actually proved to be relatively tame - even though everybody came to know that villagers were helping some of the internees to escape.

Unfortunately, in the spring of 2001 we found that the passing of a further 50 years since those dark days had done nothing to help the condition of the little huddle of church buildings. Rather, the ravages of the upland climate, the poor materials which had been used in their construction, and the design and methods by which they had been assembled, had all combined to leave the structures in a parlous condition. The church itself retained much of its original, century old, Jewish decoration though with Christian symbols where those of that other faith had once been found. However, the lower walls were, like those in the apartment in Komárom, affected by damp. Their plaster was crumbling away to dust. Meanwhile, the concrete floor was thin and cracked and let water in. The windows were single glazed despite outside temperatures often falling to -30 degrees Celsius or below each winter, and their frames were ill-fitting, admitting icy draughts. The venerable fixed pews were uncomfortable in the extreme and lacked any kind of appeal, particularly to younger generations.

Yes, the total effect was certainly picturesque, but also very inflexible indeed, and unattractive to anyone who had not grown up in the church. Most seriously of all, the mud brick walls of the adjoining set of small function rooms were both naturally weak and burdened by massive roofs. No wonder they showed signs of imminent collapse!

When Tim accompanied us to Recsk in June to plan in detail the September campaign, he found yet another problem, potentially the most serious of them all. Unlike the other walls of the church which were more strongly constructed of stone, the inner wall between the sanctuary and its neighbouring room was made of mud brick. If the dangerous outbuildings were to be demolished, this mud brick wall would be immediately exposed to the rain, snow and frost that were already wreaking such havoc with some of the other buildings. If they collapsed, in true domino style the worship area would then be jeopardised too!

Together with Pastor Imre, his wife Erika, and church members Peter and Dániel, a plan of action was drawn up. We left funds to enable a new concrete floor to be lain before our return in September with our Seventh Team. Replacement window frames would also be have to be made to await our arrival. Then we would fit them, complete with special 'trickle vents' which we would bring from England to help the ventilation of the building. They would be taken out on our ground support minibus, along with a large quantity of Hammerite with which to repaint the long lengths of railings enclosing the church plot, and protect them from further rusting.

And what can we say of that September Practical Mission itself? Afterwards top Team carpenter Howard summed up everything in just three succinct words: "THE BEST YET!" - though I myself recall times in the thick of the battle when he, at least, could have been excused for temporarily not thinking that. One such occasion had been on our trip to timber yards in the nearby town of Eger. As usual in Hungary it proved difficult, if not impossible, to find matching cuts of wood, particularly fully seasoned ones which were also straight enough for our purposes. Howard's wry verdict at the time was that most of the stock seemed to have come from banana trees!

Fortunately, buying the paint we needed was easier, though most of this, in normal east European fashion, had to be hand mixed. This is always an interesting challenge, not least because from the outset enough has to be made up for each task. No two mixes concocted from: "A drop or two of this, and a drop or two of that," could ever emerge from the can the same.

Even before the painting stage there was, of course, a more fundamental question to be resolved: "Once the walls have been cleaned and repaired, what new colour scheme should we use for the interior of the church? This decision had to be taken by Tim and myself, in consultation with Erika, to whom Pastor Imre was usually glad to defer on such matters. For a couple of days we had no good ideas about this.

In the meantime, fast progress was being made with the preparatory work on the walls themselves. Terry, Dave and Imre replastered the damp-affected lower parts, then Jim and Andrew began battening them prior to fitting new plasterboard panels to a height of about three feet. Howard, Terry and Dave fitted the new set of trickle-vented window frames with their vital new, double glazed glass, and the painting gang of Mike, another Tim, Tom and Cathy attacked those great lengths of outside railings. Gillian, Jo and I, while not on shopping trips or kitchen chores, helped with these too.

In Hungary for the first time since accompanying SGA Field Representative Derek Vigurs to that country all of 20 years earlier, Derek's unexpectedly early homecall to Heaven, David quietly but efficiently beavered away on the lighting of the church interior. The final *piéces de resistance* of the new *décor* proved to be a stunning pair of modern candelabras with multiple purple lampshades, which I had spotted in a store in Eger. David also had the pleasure of fitting them too. Yet again like Nehemiah's practical minion's of old, all ours worked with a will to ensure that everything would be much more God-honouring in the future than it had been in the recent past.

But what colour scheme should be chosen? The need to answer this vital question was becoming very pressing. Suddenly, inspiration came from a most unexpected source. Maybe this is even unique in the whole history of church decorating: the tracksuit the pastor's wife was wearing! One morning Erika looked specially fetching in her two-tone blue outfit, and in a flash we realised that the church would look good in those colours too!

Thus the white upper walls and ceilings came to be nicely anchored by two-tone blue panelling at their bases, set off by purple beading to key in with those candelabras we had loved as soon as we had spotted them in the Eger store. Finished with a floor of new, dominantly white ceramic tiles, plus further blue trim around the removable partition which Howard and his gang had erected to provide a cry room at the back of the sanctuary, the total effect was very pleasing. It was crisp, clean yet suitably restrained for a modern place of worship.

Because the century-old pews would have looked very out of place in the renovated church, we ordered sets of new chairs to complete the picture, though Gillian and I were not to see them in place until we returned briefly in November. Fifty are dark blue upholstered ones, twenty purplish blue plastic ones, and eight pale blue plastic kiddies' seats, all of which we had also seen and liked in Eger. Together with the other changes, the new seating has helped transform the church from the cold, damp, uncomfortable and inflexible antique it had been to a much warmer, drier, brighter and more welcoming one, whose seating can be rearranged to suit the needs of each occasion.

Exceptionally, we had allowed Mike's children, Tom and Cathy, to join us on the Seventh Team, for the dates of the Practical Missions almost always embrace their birthdays. "You can only go again this year," they had said to their Dad, "if you take us too!"

So, on the last evening before our overland group were due to set out for home, and along with many local friends, we gathered in the new room behind the removable partition at the back of the church for a time of special celebration. Not only did we praise God together for the wonderful week we had had serving Him so practically, but we also marked Tom and Cathy's anniversaries with a birthday tea, complete with two large, specially ordered cream layer cakes.

Just six weeks later, Gillian and I succumbed to a pressing invitation from Imre and Erika to return to Hungary and Recsk for the rededication of the chapel. It was a glorious late autumn day as we wound round the switchback bends of 'The Snake', intently following all its twists and turns around Mount Kékestető. Under the cobalt blue, cloudless sky the dense beechwoods of the Mátras were richly bedecked with gold and bronze. Between the close packed trunks the sloping forest floors glinted as sunbeams burnished the thickening carpets of fallen yellow leaves.

As we approached the little church we exulted in its own smart, clean appearance, as bright as the proverbial new pin, and marvelled at the extra work the tiny band of local men had put in since we had been there so recently, by further tidying and smartening the compound. Even the inner courtyard leading to the main entrance on one side had been spruced up beyond all recognition.

Inside the church, the floor tiling which our Team had not had time to finish was all in place, topped off by rows of the new chairs we had ordered. To our great surprise two flags adorned the frame of the new removable partition, one of them the red, green and white tricolour of Hungary... and the other the Union Jack! But we appreciated this symbolic touch, for as on every Practical Mission we had worked closely with our Hungarian friends to bring about all those improvements which they would never have been able to achieve alone.

And were our Mátra friends pleased with the results of our joint labours on their patch? Oh yes, A thousand times YES! In Recsk that weekend in November 2001 folk packed in from all six of Imre and Erika's little mountain congregations, along with a special choir from the city of Miskolc, to praise and thank God for His unexpected grace and goodness to them. Merely nine months earlier He had known of the forthcoming, freely-to-be-provided attention to the premises of their central church, but they had not.

The selfsame János we had known so well from his Győr pastoral days is now the Mission Director for the Hungarian Baptist Union. As earlier related in Chapter 1, he finally arrived at the very last minute to give the main address in the first of the two three-hour long Thanksgiving Services that weekend. In doing so he stressed how much the help given by our Team had encouraged the whole of Imre's circuit in that remote upland area.

As János was speaking, my mind wandered back to the time in the spring when I had first spoken to Erika on the phone - and found myself recalling the unusual directions she had given to help us find the church and their house next door.

"In the village you will pass the school on the right. It is the only building with two floors. Then, at a small crossroads, turn right. Look for a garden with a yellow fence that needs painting, and in the garden a poor little dog with a broken leg!"

Armed only with those strange instructions we had set out from Gyöngyös, wondering if we would ever find the right place. Yet we had, first go. Talking to János after the Saturday afternoon Thanksgiving Service, and hearing his explanation for his delayed arrival, I reflected with some amusement that we had even found it more easily than he had done, despite his having been there several times before!

But surely János could be forgiven for driving straight past, for like all the other places where our remarkable Practical Teams have worked so hard to help build structures evocative of eternity, had not this one in Recsk been changed, almost out of ALL RECOGNITION...!?

CHAPTER 5

THE FLIPCHART FLURRY

"I'm very happy," smiled the dark-haired, brown-eyed young woman at the front of the crowded little church, "to be able to give you this set of Flipchart Books to help the children of Komárom learn more of the love God has for every one of them!"

Her older sister, Joli accepted the gifts graciously - and the two of them embraced with a warm hug, and the traditional Hungarian kiss on either cheek.

In every sense these were tear-jerking moments, and I had to surreptitiously wipe my eyes before getting back to my feet and proceeding with my message that Sunday morning service in Komárom Baptist Church in late May 2002. For was not this an occasion I had been anticipating with special eagerness since I had last visited that Fellowship something over one year before...?

****

Early one Sunday morning in early April 2001, Gillian and I had woken in an 'outback' village in the *Nagyalföld*, the Great Plain of central and eastern Hungary, to find thickly falling snow whitening the whole landscape. For us that late snowfall had been a pretty but unwelcome sight, for a long drive lay ahead of us that morning if we were to be in Komárom - 120 miles away on the north-west border of Hungary - hopefully in time for the morning service beginning at half-past nine.

Fortunately, and unlike at home in North Somerset in similar weather conditions, we found that even the side roads to that village had been freshly cleared of snow. So, once we had carefully crunched our way the first few hundred yards along the unmade up track which ran past the house where we had been staying, our progress had been reasonably good. The weather and the roads further improved as we headed north towards Budapest. The M3, M0 and M1 motorways we then took in sequence were even clear of any blowing snow.

Still, we were slightly breathless as we drew up outside the humble *imaház* or prayer house which was our destination. It was smartly adorned in the new coats of paint our Sixth Practical Team had applied to its exterior just six months before. There were only five minutes to spare before the service was due to begin, so we touched base quickly with Pastor Zsolt, who would interpret my message, and with lay evangelist Sándor, who had been such a tremendous help to our recent Sixth Team. He would be leading worship.

Once the meeting was over, we enjoyed chatting with many of the congregation whom we had come to know and love during the previous September. Then outside, just as we were preparing to accompany Sándor to lunch, we found ourselves talking to a young couple who had taken part in the service, but whom we had not seen before. Indeed, we learned this was the first time they had been to that church. Gábor, the husband, had played the keyboard very well, and his young wife Joli had said a few words at one point in the proceedings. Because these had not been translated for us, they had remained something of a mystery.

"We're here 'with a view' to becoming the new young people's workers," Gábor explained, "so if we joined the church, we would be living in the apartment on which your Team worked last year."

Then Joli added, unexpectedly: "I have a sister, Noémi, who is an *au pair* in England. She's in a place called Knowle, Bristol. Do you know it?"

Gillian and I gasped in unison. "OF COURSE we know it! For many years we lived only three miles from there, and still only live 12 miles away today. As soon as we get home, we will make a date for Noémi to come to ours for lunch."

So Joli gave us her sister's address and telephone number in Bristol, and we left wondering whether Noémi might just possibly be the answer to a prayer we had recently begun to pray....

****

During the few weeks prior to leaving home on that particular visit to Hungary we had been given a set of newly published children's ministry resource materials. These were in the shape of large-format 'Flipchart Books' for schools and Sunday Schools, along with accompanying notes for the teachers who would be using them. At that time there were six different books in the Bible-based series: three on the Easter story, and one each on other topics entitled: *The Bread of Life, The Good Shepherd* and *Who is My Neighbour? - The Story of the Good Samaritan*. Each A3-sized book tells its story through nine or ten specially drawn colour plates, with captions summarising the action in each one.

On giving us a set of the flipchart books, our friend Priscilla had remarked: "I wonder if these would be of any use in Hungary?"

By the time we reached Komárom a few weeks later, we had already gleaned several responses to that interesting question.

One had been from Attila and Erzsébét in Kőszeg: "They're beautiful!" they remarked. "We don't have ANYTHING like these in Hungary!"

This had come as no surprise to us for, in the years of freedom following the end of the communist era, any slender local resources available for printing projects had been spent on perceived higher priorities: Bibles, concordances, hymn books, and devotional books, generally in that order. Materials for Sunday Schools and Bible Clubs - or 'Bible Circles' as both were commonly known in Hungary - have not been highly prioritised, so the general need for these is now all the greater.

A second response was from Josef and Wendy in Pápa. Theirs was particularly interesting, for they also know the British situation: "These flipcharts are the best we have ever seen, " they warmly enthused.

Yet another reaction came from Károly and Ágnes in Orgovány. They are key Hungarian national and international workers of whom much more will be said in later chapters. In the early 1990s they established a charity of their own called *Örömhír Alapítvány*, the Good News Foundation, one of whose chief functions is to prepare and provide aids to workers among children and young people throughout the Hungarian speaking world. On first seeing the flipchart books,"WE COULD USE 100 SETS TOMORROW!" was their somewhat stunning response.

Therefore, even as we had headed north towards Komárom on that snowy morning in early April 2001, Gillian and I had been praying that the Lord would direct us to a good translator for the flipchart materials. There was clearly such a strong demand for them!

It would be necessary, too, for the translator to be prepared to undertake that considerable task voluntarily, for we had no budget for such a project at that time. We were not even sure how much each set of Flipchart Books might cost, and how many we might be able to afford. However, as the Apostle Paul observed on one occasion: *"We live by faith, not by sight..."* (2 Corinthians 5:7), and knew that if the Lord was in this notion, then He would help ensure that the necessary cash would become available, and in His own good time.

So as Joli told us about her sister, who lived so near our home when she might have been anywhere in England from Penzance to Berwick-on-Tweed, we had wondered if Noémi might just prove to be God's chosen way of meeting that related, specific, and perhaps even more pressing need: for someone to help with the flipchart translations...?

****

One week after hearing of Noémi I picked her up from the house in Knowle, Bristol where she was au pairing, and headed back to our home a few miles away for lunch and afternoon tea. Some time afterwards we learnt that she had phoned home that evening saying: "I never thought that I would have such a good day!"

For her part, she was fascinated by all we could tell and show of our involvement in churches in her own country. Together we were delighted to discover that we had many mutual friends in Hungary. Some of these were originally from her own home town, despite its remote location down near the south-east border with Rumania, a region we had not yet visited ourselves. And Gillian and I marvelled at Noémi's account of that same morning when we had heard of her through Joli.

"Some people I had recently met took me for the first time to your church in Bristol," she explained. "In the morning service they talked about the couple who were in Hungary, and prayed for your ministry as you were speaking in Komárom Baptist Church. I was so excited to hear this that I told the pastor afterwards: 'THAT'S THE CHURCH WHERE MY SISTER AND HER HUSBAND ARE VISITING TODAY!' After that, I looked forward so much to meeting you!"

In response to that startling news, I recalled hearing of a Christian who had come under scornful attack from a non-Christian friend for believing that God actually hears and answers the prayers of His people: "It's nothing but coincidence!" this man had scoffed.

"Then how do you explain the fact that when I don't pray, COINCIDENCES NEVER SEEM TO HAPPEN?" the Christian pertinently replied.

Certainly Gillian, Noémi and I were all struck by the wonderful 'coincidence' whereby at virtually the same time, on the same day, more than one thousand miles apart and with no special planning by any of us, we had heard of Noémi and she had heard of us. We were convinced, and remain convinced today, that this was one of those amazing answers to prayer that so encourage us to be sure that He is in control of our lives. He has His own special ways of determining that His strategic purposes are carried out!

The next twelve months abundantly confirmed that it was indeed the Lord who had planned for Noémi and us to do much together. Had we met earlier it might have been too soon, for she was on a quite steep English language learning curve. We were glad to be able to help her immediately with this through regular English lessons, and support for some of her college courses. In turn, we soon began to reap the benefits through her translation work on the flipcharts, and other things she readily agreed to do with us. I particularly appreciated the help she began to give in many of our regular deputation meetings, for I was strongly constrained to continue with these even after Gillian's brain tumour was diagnosed on 3 February 2002, as Chapter 10 will further explain. Following her five-hour intercranial brain surgery just two days later, Gillian was only able to attend and participate in another handful of our deputation meetings. So, until Noémi's return to Hungary in late May, it was she who came with me to services whenever she could, which was to most of them through the next four months.

In all of those meetings Noémi looked after the literature table, and in most of them I found it helpful to interview her too, bringing a breath of authentic Hungarian fresh air to the proceedings. Everywhere people responded really well not only to her lovely accent, but even more to her warm smile, sunny personality and obvious desire to serve the Lord. In those interviews we would not only talk about the flipchart project, but we were also able to flesh out a little more fully the mental images our prayer partners had of the lives of churches and Christians in the Hungarian region of central and eastern Europe. In some ways all the countries which were once behind the old Iron Curtain are now more like our own than they were... but there are still both obvious, and less than obvious, ways in which life there is very different. So, one of my interviews with Noémi went something like this:

"Noémi, we're so glad to have you with us today! First tell us your full name, and where you come from."

"My name is Veres Noémi - in Hungary we always put the family name first. My home is in Békés, a town in south east Hungary. Its name means 'peace'. I think that's rather nice."

"Tell us, what does your father do?"

"He is a pastor, of four churches, but also grows vegetables, especially tomatoes, cucumbers and potatoes."

"You mean in the back garden, for the family?"

"Oh no! He grows them to make a living, because all his churches are small, and too poor to pay him for being their pastor. We have two big greenhouses of our own, and my grandparents next door have ten more. Dad helps with them too."

"Noémi, you've touched on something many people in the UK may not realise: not just your Dad's churches, but MOST of them in eastern and central Europe are too poor to be able to pay their pastors. So these are what we would call 'lay' pastors. That's why some Western missions like our own do all they can to help some of the denominational leaders, pastors and church planters financially - so they can spend more time than otherwise on the Lord's work, and less on trying to balance their family budgets. But you spoke of your greenhouses: are they like the little one I have in my garden?"

"Definitely not! Ours are VERY BIG, maybe 3 metres high, and 90 metres long!"

"Wow! That's some 10 feet tall, and about one hundred yards from end to end. That's not just big, but ENORMOUS! Together they must cover the greater part of a football field. It must be really hard work looking after them?"

"Yes, it is, and we all help. My mother has back problems from carrying heavy boxes of tomatoes and cucumbers. Full ones weigh 35 kilograms - that's 77 pounds in the British system, isn't it? But she has to do it, so Dad can continue to teach people about God."

"Let me see 77 pounds... that's two-thirds of Gillian's weight. If your Mother is lifting these, I'm not at all surprised that she has problems with her back! And as far as your father is concerned, he must have a very busy life - a sort of 'cucumber-and-church sandwich'?"

"Yes, exactly! He has to get up very early every weekday morning especially when things have to go to market. Also, our churches are all in different villages, so every Sunday he drives over 160 kilometres to visit them. Then there are midweek meetings to lead, and visiting to be done."

"And what of you, Noémi? When did you first hear the Gospel, and when did you become a Christian?"

"Being a pastor's daughter, I guess I heard the Bible message as soon as I was born. When I was about nine years old I trusted Jesus Christ as my own Saviour, and was baptised soon afterwards."

"I know you're very good with children. You've worked with them already, in Hungary as well as here in England?"

"Yes, I love children. In Knowle I have been helping as a classroom assistant, and in Hungary the Baptists have a camp near Budapest. In the summer holidays you could say I grew up there, going every year. Then, in the last year or two, I've become a helper with the children's groups. I really enjoy all that."

"Soon you will be returning to Hungary permanently, after two years here, to take the next big steps in your life: either beginning university studies or going out to work. So, thank you for sharing with us today and we wish you God's richest blessing in everything you go on to do for Him!"

At that point I would pause to let Noémi sit down again, before continuing to address the audience: "Isn't it <u>wonderful</u> how God, one of whose names is *Jehovah Jireh'*- the 'Lord Provides' - meets His people's needs when they seek to live for Him? When we knew we needed a translator for the flipchart materials we thought of the characteristics such a person would need to have. He or she would have to be a Christian Believer, and know the Bible well. They would need to know English as well as Hungarian, and how to understand children and communicate with them. They would also have to have time to do the job, and feel called of the Lord to do it. Noémi fits all of these criteria in full. We <u>thank God</u> for so amazingly bringing her and us together... and Noémi, WE THANK YOU SO MUCH for the many hours you have sacrificially spent on this project, so conscientiously and cheerfully completed!"

****

Those 'many hours' spread over virtually a whole year after we met Noémi in April 2001. And many more hours were spent on the same project by Geoff and Sue from nearby Clevedon. They are the hearts, brains and souls of New Generation Productions, being the originators and publishers of the Flipchart Book series. Warmly and graciously they endorsed our vision of a Hungarian-language version of their products and, along with Noémi and ourselves worked long and hard to ensure that no practical obstacle would stand in the way. Specially tricky was to be the word-processing to fit the different-length Hungarian captions into the spaces available on the English picture pages, which we had decided to over-paste with the replacement ones. To have specially printed a relatively small batch of charts in the new language would have been prohibitively expensive. However, finding the best medium on which to print the Hungarian wording was also quite a challenge, not least because none of the readily available materials were sufficiently opaque. With many gummed labels 'print-through' is all too evident.

After much trial and error, Geoff discovered a product appropriately called *Crack-a-Back*. This is a white paper with a pale blue underlay to eliminate print-through. It also has a strong adhesive backing which is covered, until use, by a peel-off layer. But even when this quite sophisticated stuff had been printed with the

Hungarian titles and captions, two other related problems had to be overcome. One was how to cope with the 7,000-plus captions which needed to be pasted over the 360 flipcharts we could afford at that time. Geoff and Sue did some practice runs and reckoned that the whole task would take one reasonably nimble-fingered person well over 100 hours. Clearly we alone could not undertake the whole of such a mammoth task! The other problem was how best to do the sticking itself so as to ensure a minimum of wastage. We soon recognised that any individual caption, if pasted poorly, could spoil a whole Flipchart Book.

The only reasonable solution to the basic challenge seemed to be to use the proverbial many hands to make light work of the task, even though a few who volunteered might struggle to achieve the quality the work demanded. It was agreed that I would organise one team of stickers, and Geoff would organise another. Each team would spend one evening on the job at a conveniently chosen local church.

Subsequently, with the help of Geoff and Sue, plus some 50 friends in total from a dozen different fellowships, the two super sticking sessions which ensued at North Somerset churches in Claverham and Yatton proved to be great successes. We heard no-one say affectionately: "*Crack-a-back* is something we could really get attached to!" for there were certainly some sore and sticky fingers before those evenings ended. Furthermore, unexpectedly exploited muscles also started to complain, and eyes soon ached from unaccustomed concentration. But, with the exception of a few flipchart 'hospital cases' which Geoff and Sue nobly offered to nurse back to health afterwards, almost all our stock was successfully adorned by the end of the second of those sessions. Better still, it was clear that everyone had enjoyed working on that project which was destined to help bring God's Word to life for thousands of Hungarian speaking children in several countries through the next few years.

Maybe my own most abiding memory of those two unique times of Christian service and fellowship is permanently preserved in one snapshot of Noémi. She is happily holding up one of the final flipchart captions just about to be stuck securely into place. There is such a broad, beaming smile on her face as she sees all her own meticulous translation work finally coming to fruition!

"This has been one of the best times of my life," Noémi exclaimed, so encouraged to find how many British people had been ready to lend their hands to help with that last important flipchart project push. Merely one week later she was on her way home to Hungary for good: as usual the Lord's timing throughout this effort had been both precise and perfect.

****

A further two weeks after the sticking session, I flew out to Hungary myself. Sadly, Gillian was not well enough to accompany me as the doctors had earlier hoped. When it became obvious three or four days before the flights that she would not be able to travel, I contacted the Dutch airline KLM, with whom we had both been booked to fly from Bristol to Budapest via Amsterdam. Explaining the situation, I related how we had planned to take the first dozen of the flipchart sets with us, and to economise on our own personal baggage so as to stay within our free weight allowance. Now I was to travel alone, the flipcharts would exceed my own allowance, leaving me without even a change of socks! Explaining this to the airline, I pointed out that I had purchased two tickets - both boldly endorsed 'NON-REFUNDABLE' - and asked if, in Gillian's absence, I could therefore be permitted to use her free baggage allowance too?

The Customer Relations Department of KLM was sympathetic, but at best non-committal: "We cannot make any such promise," they replied. "It is unlikely, and all depends on the supervisor at the airport on the morning of travel."

That, of course, was the last answer I had wanted to hear! How could I pack my own personal things under such a cloud of uncertainty? And how could I finalise my travel plans inside Hungary, without knowing whether I could take all the flipcharts I had planned or not?

On check-in, though, I found my urgent prayers had been positively answered. The supervisor was in a cheerful mood: "We have a larger plane on that service this morning," she informed me. "So it has nine spare seats on board, and we will let you take 50 kilos of luggage without extra charge."

Considering that the normal allowance is merely 20 kilos, I was astonished and overjoyed. Even better still, the previous evening I had already received another, and totally unexpected, cause for thankfulness to God. Quite out of the blue I had received a fax from the Ticket Reimbursement Office of KLM. In a nutshell, it had said that, in the circumstances of my wife's illness, they were arranging for her ticket to be reimbursed in full!

To this day I remain flabbergasted by this. Because of the 'NON-REFUNDABLE' endorsement on her ticket, I had not even bothered to ask if a refund might be possible. And in any case, it would have been unusual for this to be total. I had also been aware of how I had had to negotiate a refund for such a ticket on Gillian's behalf earlier in the year from our travel insurance company, and so could not have claimed the same again because of her 'existing condition'. No, the £208 her ticket had cost was money I had completely written off.

To this day I do not know how, in human terms, the appropriate KLM department heard of this problem. I do know, though, that their gesture was as much appreciated as it was - from a commercial point of view - unnecessary.

However, I was very soon to discover that the Lord had had His own purposes for that money, so unexpectedly returned to me by the airline's splendid gesture....

****

Three days after travelling out to Hungary, on Sunday 23 May 2002 I witnessed along with the congregation in Komárom Baptist Church that tear-jerking moment with which this chapter opened. How fitting it was that Joli's church should be the first to receive a flipchart set... and that Noémi herself should be there to make the presentation! Events had conspired to enable Noémi to be the perfect travelling companion for me that week in Gillian's absence. I could so easily have been resigned to making my ten day trip alone, but instead Noémi had insisted she should accompany me as interpreter, companion and co-driver. Better still, she came with her father's Lada car, so that I would not have to rent. Although over 30 years old, running on liquid petroleum gas, and with its Polish origin symbolically betrayed by its Cyrillic script dashboard instruments, it ran well throughout, and never remotely felt like breaking down.

But before we moved on from Komárom for our next destination I was ecstatic for another reason too. Prior to the service when the flipchart presentation was to be made I had been enjoying a quick cup of tea in Joli and Gábor's kitchen, part of that church apartment which our Sixth Team had helped renovate twenty months before. Suddenly I became aware that Joli, seven months pregnant with their second child, was standing nearby, leaning with her back against the wall.

"Why don't you sit down, Joli?" I enquired solicitously. "Can I get you a chair?"

"We haven't any to spare," came the unexpected answer. "They are all in the young people's room. We get so many coming now that they need all the chairs we can find."

Later that day I lunched with evangelist Sándor and his wife Ággie in the apartment they now live in with their two young children. They had waited several years for it. The flat is in a former Russian army barracks building, and though unfinished, is for them: "Home, sweet home!" as Sándor happily put it. All at once an idea sparked in my mind.

My memory skipped back to the previous autumn, and the three sets of chairs we had bought in Eger for the renovated church at Recsk. We had been able to get nicely padded, metal-framed chairs for about £10 each, much cheaper than the same kind would be in the UK. But those chairs had been 'on special'. I wondered, could any be obtained in the Komárom area for a similar price?

"How many chairs do you think you could buy for £208?" I found myself asking my hosts. "I was concerned that Joli only had one in her apartment this morning - and I myself was sitting on that!"

Ággie sought out a recent catalogue. We scanned it eagerly. "Yes," she exclaimed, "it looks as if we could buy 20 for that sum!" In that moment I gave thanks to God for the unexpected rebate on Gillian's air ticket. I marvelled yet again at the delightful truth of Psalm 25:10 that: *"The ways of the Lord are loving and faithful."* His methods are SO MUCH MORE AMAZING than our own. With what wonderful imagination God plans to satisfy the needs of His children!

Soon after returning home I received an email from Sándor and Ággie. *"As we promised,"* it ran, in Sándor's almost-correct English, *"we spent the kind gift you left for chairs. You may see it on the attached file's picture. We have bought twenty piece of these kinds of chairs. We are very happy with them! Thank you so very much once again...."*

But even that was still not quite the end of the story, for in October I was briefly back in Komárom on my way from Vienna to Bicske, nearer Budapest. I was glad to see that Joli and Gábor now had more than one chair in their kitchen. However, glancing into the young people's room, I was a little surprised to see what appeared to be old pews arranged around the walls. "Where are the new chairs?" I asked Sándor who had come over from work to see me.

"Oh," he smiled, and ushered me into the neat little sanctuary. They're all in here. Some of the older members of the congregation thought they were much too good for the teenagers... and in any case the young people said they would prefer the old pews, because they would not have to be so careful with them. So here are the chairs, and everyone is so happy with you, and KLM!"

****

As can be imagined, my multipurpose visit to Hungary in May and June 2002, so providentially accompanied by Noémi, saw flipchart sets safely delivered not only to Komárom, but to several other places too. More happy tears were surreptitiously shed the following Sunday near the Rumanian border in Magyarhomorog, where the largest church her father pastors is located. In the morning service I was formally welcomed by the leader of the local Parish Council, and serenaded by a choir of children specially trained to sing for their rare English visitor. Then Noémi, who also interpreted for me when I preached, made her presentation of a set of flipchart books to that group of churches - through her pastor Dad. At that point several hankies were in evidence in the congregation - including mine!

And there was a similarly touching moment when she gave a set to the pastor of her large home church in the town of Békés during one Friday evening meeting. Would not any fellowship be glad to see one of its young people being so useful to the Lord, particularly when only 21 years old?

On that ministry tour, other flipchart sets were left in two churches in the town of Jászberény, 50 miles east of Budapest. As the next chapter will explain, I had spent some time there earlier in the year, when the Reformed and Bible Baptist churches had memorably joined forces to arrange a series of outreach talks which I had given. The pastors of those two churches, Pastor Róbért and Pastor Jerry respectively, received us and our gifts with grace and gladness.

Then, on a beautiful, sparkling, sunny morning we drove on further to Gyöngyös, where SGA-supported church planters Jonatón and Örsi are so imaginatively ministering... before wriggling up and round the fabled hairpins of 'The Snake'. These led again through the beautiful beechwoods of Mount Kékesteto - now lime green in all the freshness of their early summer foliage - and on to Recsk, to revisit the church our Seventh Team had so successfully restored the previous autumn.

That little church will always have special memories for me, for it was the last in Hungary that Gillian would ever see. It was still as bright as a button in its fetching new colour scheme of blue, white and purple, just as I remembered it from the rededication services in November. "And the church was so lovely and WARM in the winter!" Erika exclaimed as we showed Noémi round.

After giving Imre and Erika a set of flipcharts to be shared with their six Mátra congregations, we also had the chance to show some to the Pastor's Conference that had been arranged while we were there. Nine ministers from the north-east region assembled for this. It was good to see the more flexible space we had helped create being put to such an appropriate use - and to find that almost all the pastors were keen to receive flipcharts on behalf of the children's work leaders in their own churches.

Last but not least on that tour it was a pleasure to see Károly and Ágnes once more in their Good News Foundation headquarters in Orgovány. There will be much more to write about them and their work in a later chapter - plus the plans we were to draw up together in October 2002 to cover a much wider range of publications and resource materials for distribution throughout the various countries in the Hungarian speaking world. Suffice it to say for the moment that it is through the Good News Foundation that most of the other 50 sets of flipchart books for which funds were forthcoming are being distributed. What kinds of churches are involved? In addition to the Baptist, Bible Baptist and Lutheran churches already mentioned, flipcharts are now with Evangelical, Gypsy, Pentecostal and home churches too, across the whole of Hungary as well as in neighbouring Serbia, Slovakia, Rumania and Ukraine.

And how have the flipcharts been distributed so widely? Is it not difficult and costly to spread anything over such an extensive region? No, because the Lord has already provided for the flipcharts and subsequent items to be sent to all the churches free of charge! As Károly told us with a twinkle, two members of the Good News Fellowship which meets in their home are employed by the Hungarian Postal Service. They have a perk that their British counterparts do not, and which they envy: Hungarian postal workers can send anything through the post to Hungary or its 'next-door neighbours' for no cost at all. In a country where money is so scarce, especially for the Lord's work, this is just another of the many little ways in which He encourages His children, and enables His Word to be spread around.

And the provision of the sets of flipcharts themselves as free gifts from us in the UK is a great encouragement, for most churches in the Hungarian world simply do not have the resources to buy things like these beautifully produced aids.

****

So, is the *'Flipchart Flurry'* - the hectic burst of sudden flipchart-related activity which the period from early 2001 to late 2002 specially witnessed - now at an end? No, it is not! Geoff and Sue are adding to their range of titles, and their new one entitled *'Teach Me to Pray'* came into my hands in December 2002. Translation of the captions and leader's notes was quickly completed by Noémi away in Hungary, and funds already to hand were sufficient to ensure that a copy could go to every one of the 60 churches which had received the first six.

Friends in Hungary join us in hoping that they will be able to receive other new issues too, for response to these aids to teaching the Christian message has been so positive. Excerpts from early feedback have included these:

"I have been praying for the children's work at our church for several years.... We desperately needed illustrative materials of a high standard. The flipchart set is a perfect gift from our Heavenly Father. Thank you for your work from God!"

+++

"This is really precious material! Its execution is accurate, aesthetic, thorough and shone through by your love, your carefulness, and care which transfer blessing.... We really appreciate your help, and we strive to take care of these flipcharts in order to use it long time and in proper way."

+++

"In connection with our Sunday School one year ago we started this, but actually it was just looking after children. When more came, it became necessary to teach them. There were some people enthusiastically working, but they missed a direction to follow. Now we have some very nice, demanding and useful things to help. We organise a training for the teachers, to help them do their best."

+++

"It was the RIGHT TIME when I got the flipchart set! At my school where I work among handicapped children I have been asked to pass on my annual plan of subjects. By these materials the Gospel can be introduced. It is a big help for me now, and in the future in children's evangelism."

+++

"Thank you so much for the flipcharts! It is a very good idea! I can even use this in my family. I can teach my cousins, and in my friendships. May God bless you, and all who help to make this possible!"

+++

Such highly positive responses mirror and extend those already witnessed in the UK itself, where sales of the original English versions have been made to many state schools as well as churches and other Christian organisations.

Surely, in the years ahead many Believers, and even some church leaders, in that region of Europe will be able to assert: "It was the presentation of the Bible message by those flipcharts that first really captured our imagination, and set us on our personal paths of faith in Jesus Christ."

In the meantime it is our prayer that this will be so. And the routes and connections that have been opened up for the flipchart project both in the UK and 'on the field' are already being followed again for other much-needed Hungarian-language books and resource materials, as Chapter 7 will explain....

CHAPTER 6

HIGHER HURDLES

There are times when we all find it relatively easy to respond to God's call, and some when we do not.

Looking back, I an somewhat amused to see that almost all my Christian life I have been constrained by the Lord to do things I earlier vowed I would never do.

The first major 'personal reluctance hurdle' I had real difficulty clearing after becoming a Christian at age twelve was <u>Believer's baptism</u>: a high hurdle indeed for a mildly hydrophobic non-swimmer like me! The very thought of having my head plunged under water even for a few seconds filled me with dread, and it was to take me some ten years before I could bring myself to 'take the plunge'. By that time I was so ashamed of myself that the service was arranged over 200 miles away from my home.

Then there was the <u>preaching</u> hurdle. By nature I was, and still am, a person who from preference would not be in the public eye. However, by the time I was 20 that hurdle had been cleared already. When I reported this to my mother, she responded: "Oh...but I recall you saying so many times, 'You will never get <u>me</u> in the pulpit!"

All I could say in reply was: "Well, I was right. You never could. It was THE LORD who did!"

And, of course, that was the truth of the matter.

The third major personal hurdle that I would not have crossed if I had had my own way was even higher than those other two. In short, I had no personal interest in becoming involved in addressing the <u>interface between science and the Christian faith</u>. For one thing

I have always remained conscious of my humble family background. Linked with this is my still continuing wish to be able to relate to people for whom intellectual debate is either impossible because of their educational level, or anathema because it is all so hypothetical. Additionally, I have always been very conscious of the truth of the old adage in academic Christian circles that: *"It is easy to grow colder by degrees!"*

No, I have long preferred that the daily outworking of my Christian faith should be much more practical than theoretical. The Practical Mission projects are just one confirmation that this wish is still alive and well!

Thus, for more years than I care to count, I did my very best to avoid bringing together my scientific work - which I have always basically viewed as an interesting means of making more important things in life possible - and the public ministries I now know I am called to engage in whether I wish to or not. In particular I have long disliked the very thought of Christian scientific apologetics, the pompous name for attempts to justify the Bible and the Christian faith by means of scientific evidence and argument. No, I particularly never wanted to become involved in things like this.

For the first decade or so of my university lecturing career I successfully managed to steer clear of most such matters, though often times I found myself wondering: "Why have I not been called to 'full-time' Christian service?"

Sometimes it is very hard to preach, undertake missionary deputation and help 'on the field' when there is a demanding professional job to be done first. Surely, I reasoned, to be a full time Christian worker might be easier…?

Then, inch by painful inch, the Lord began to coax me towards that science-and-Christian-faith hurdle I had not wanted to face. In Chapter 1, reference was made to Joseph Steiner, so long the only voice of the Gospel to Hungary from Trans World Radio, and how Gillian and I had got to know him so well through our early visits to its Christian radio studios in Monte Carlo. From the outset of our friendship Joseph came across as one of those very rare people who look mild and harmless on the surface, but who, given half a chance, naturally drop high-explosive depth charges after which life for those in the firing line can never be the same again.

Joseph knew how I was making my living in what a university colleague had once described as: "A rather obscure area of natural science". So, in the early 1970s he asked if I would write some short items for his Hungarian broadcasts, using scientific facts and discoveries to illustrate simple truths of the Gospel. I listened politely to the examples he gave of what he had in mind, but promptly and deliberately dismissed them from my thinking and did nothing in response to his request for help.

However, the next such invitation I received of a similar nature was to prompt the first little spark of positive reaction on my part. Early in 1974 the Rev. Peter Deyneka Jr. son of the founder of SGA, and soon to be its director himself, stayed briefly with us in our home in Bristol to speak in some meetings we had arranged for him.

"You really ought to write some scripts for our Russian language programmes, produced in our Wheaton office near Chicago," Peter remarked. "Anything that brings out the Christian message through your scientific knowledge would be very valuable, because people in the Soviet Union look up to scientists, indeed perhaps more so than to anybody else." Though Peter did not strongly press the point, I was to remember his remarks not long afterwards, far from our UK home.

At the end of May that year Gillian and I embarked on what we have since considered a completely crazy expedition to the other side of the world. This was primarily to guest lecture for one term in the University of Western Australia in Perth, but also to speak at meetings for SGA across the whole of that enormous country. Why crazy? Well, our son Andrew was only 20 months old, and our daughter Stella just ten weeks old at the time!

Armed with a carry cot for Stella and reins for Andrew we flew via Bahrain to Singapore, and then sailed down to Perth on an old rust bucket, a former Mediterranean ferry by then very inappropriately dubbed the *Eastern Queen*. The reason why we had to enter Australia by sea was because Andrew suffered from infantile eczema and could not be vaccinated against smallpox, which in those days was still endemic in certain parts of the world. By some tortuous medical logic we were told that if we took more than a week in transit on the ship, Andrew <u>might</u> be allowed into Australia if he was deemed free from smallpox when we arrived at Fremantle

Docks. Happily he was considered healthy on arrival. Whatever would we have done if the verdict had been otherwise...?!

Apparently the strain of caring for two tiny mites on such a long and arduous trip was not, for me at least, a full-time job. Happily, part of Gillian's earlier training had been as a children's nurse, for this thought was a great comfort to me. Thus, stimulated by new sights, sounds and experiences, and with some time to think when the children were asleep, I lazily began to doodle with some short word sketches on exotic things around us.

These included such unexpected topics as the distribution of the two types of grass in the little park opposite the hotel in Singapore where we had to stay two days until our departure... the stilt villages we could see from the deck of the *Eastern Queen* as our anything but regal liner at first slipped serenely through the straits between the Indonesian islands of Sumatra and Bangka... cloud patterns over the South Indian Ocean... and the remarkable, 600 foot high sand dunes down the West Australian coast. Each short script included a brief description of what I saw, followed by a summary scientific rationale, then a simple Christian application. On our arrival in Perth I posted the papers to SGA's International Office in Wheaton, Illinois - and promptly forgot all about them.

During the summer of the following year I had to fly to the Mid-Western city of Chicago in the USA, en route to the prestigious Space Science and Engineering Center in relatively nearby Madison, Wisconsin. Since Chicago's O'Hare International Airport is only 15 miles from Wheaton, I took the opportunity to touch base with colleagues and friends who were working in the American Office of SGA. One of the senior missionaries I had heard much about, but whom I then met for the first time, was Helen Zernov. Helen, a Russian by birth, had been one of the pioneers of Russian language Christian broadcasting to the Soviet Union back in the 1940s, and despite a serious heart condition was still very actively involved in it more than 30 years on.

As soon as I was introduced to Helen her blue eyes widened. "Are you the British professor who wrote those scripts about the Far East?" she enquired to my astonishment, according them and me much more respect than I thought either deserved. "I was asked to translate them into Russian. They were GREAT! Can you do some more?"

"Well," I replied, "I had not thought of doing so," but her response to those somewhat idle scribblings was so strongly positive that I knew I was being pushed closer to that hurdle I had never even wanted to approach.

The big, clearing leap was to come not long afterwards. It was the early winter of 1976. Once again Gillian and I were entertaining Peter Deyneka Jr. in our Bristol home, this time accompanied by his wife, Anita. Peter was now much more pressing than before.

"We're planning a new range of Russian language broadcasts," he explained seriously. "Each will be designed for a different type of audience: church members, women in the home, teenagers, children... and we want to include a regular programme for the more educated people of the USSR - scientists, engineers, teachers, college students and the like. These are people who particularly find atheist teaching illogical and unsatisfying. We want to introduce these thinking people to the truths and challenges of the Gospel, and also to arm Believers so they can better defend their own faith. We need a respected scientist to head this up. Will YOU?"

By this time my reluctance to consider such a proposition had already been greatly weakened. Although surprised to be asked, I was happy to discuss the possibility and begin to scope it out.

"Come to Wheaton for a year to work on it!" Peter pleaded. "We could arrange a visiting professorship for you at Wheaton College. As you know, it's only two blocks from our building, and they want to develop some more courses in environmental science. But your college workload would be light. You could spend most time with us, working up this new radio series. There would be plenty to keep you busy. You could stay with your family in one of our apartments above the offices."

My mind was racing. Glancing at Gillian for approval, I replied pensively: "I'm not sure I could get that length of leave of absence from the university just now, but maybe we could come for the summer - July until the end of September? I'd be happy to concentrate on the task through that period. I think it should be long enough, if we work hard. Could we give that a try?"

And so it was arranged. However, in the providence of God we had another foreign engagement to fulfil first. Just a few weeks later Gillian and I crossed the English Channel in our car by hovercraft, took the night car sleeper express from Paris to Nice, then drove the rest of the winding way down the west coast of Italy to Rome. There I was to work for two months as a consultant at the headquarters of the Food and Agriculture Organisation of the United Nations. My brief was to develop new satellite-based methods for monitoring a particularly long-standing threat to food crops across great swathes of the world, namely the migratory desert locust. The ultimate aim was to improve the performance of control measures against this devastating pest which formed one of the ten plagues of Egypt in the Book of Genesis, and whose life forms and their devastating effects are so graphically described in the prophecy of Joel. The insect has still been capable of causing famine and suffering ever since.

In God's economy, that preplanned stay in Rome was to be part of His preparation for me in the run up to that strategic summer in SGA/USA. In an unexpected move in the mid-1970s tens of thousands of Soviet citizens of Jewish descent were being allowed to leave the USSR. Many of them were arriving every month at a reception centre organised by the Italian government in Lido di Ostia, a seaside suburb of Rome. SGA had responded to the practical and spiritual needs of these people by opening an 'American Club' in the town to help the emigrants.

There were many opportunities to share the Gospel in 'The Club', for the newcomers all had time on their hands, and were freshly released from a country where atheism had been the official and dominant, yet deeply unsatisfying, religion. Often during that period in Rome I would take the Metro to Lido in the evenings with the family to help befriend Russian Jews in 'The Club'. On a number of unforgettable occasions I was also asked to speak to packed audiences of those intelligent, quick-witted men and women who, for once in their lives, were able to focus their minds on some of the most fundamental issues affecting every one of us on Earth.

Seeing I was a professor of environmental science, there was only one theme they wanted me to address: the one I had been so long reluctant even to contemplate, namely the relationship between science and the Christian faith. And they were exceedingly adept at asking all kinds of searching questions. Thankfully I was conscious of Holy Spirit inspiration. Thus, quite contrary to my expectations, I soon found I was actually beginning to enjoy such episodes!

So those evenings in Italy proved to be perfect training sessions for my tasks of the coming summer in the USA. Through the questions posed by the Jewish refugees from the old USSR, I was afforded priceless insights into the mindsets of an entire nation of people educated under the communist system, and the chief concerns, hopes and fears that such folk harboured. Indeed, I still cannot imagine a better training than that. The Lord is the One who, as an old Christian song neatly puts it: *"...knows the future."* It was He who had already planned my Roman mindset training when I had previously indicated to Peter and Anita that I was at last prepared to do all I could to help with the science/Christian faith programme series they wished to create.

During our family stay in Wheaton from July to September 1977 the work proceeded well. I drew up the blueprint for the new magazine-style series, and prepared an explanatory 'how-to' manual for others whom we hoped would contribute material for it. I also designed a logo and publicity brochure, and even helped produce a range of stationary for the new *Radio Academy of Science* or 'RADAS' as the project became known in the English language

To summarise, on 1 January 1980 the programme took to the air all across the vast Soviet Union, exactly following the varied 30-minute format that I had proposed. Through the next 14 years I wrote regularly for RADAS, coming to contribute about one-third of the hundreds of scripts we eventually broadcast. Many of mine were penned longhand in airport waiting lounges or aloft in the air as my scientific work took me to scores of countries all around the world. Indeed, this global work itself became another of the Lord's very special provisions for me as I strove to ensure that the programmes were as varied, interesting and international as possible.

Almost everywhere I travelled, from Alaska to Zimbabwe and from Brazil to Japan, I was able to meet with other scientists who were Christians too. I quickly came to specialise in two particular kinds of script segments: testimonies, and 'modern parables'.

In the latter, Biblical truths emerged naturally from recent scientific and technical advances, just as they had done 2000 years earlier through the parables of Jesus Christ, based so graphically on scenes from everyday life. Without my professional job-related need to travel widely it would have been far more difficult for me to help achieve many of the objectives the RADAS staff accepted for the programme as a whole.

My own scripts, once they had been translated into Russian were transmitted across the Soviet Union from several Christian short-wave radio stations around the world. They were then made available for use in other languages too, including English - and Hungarian. So the hundreds of scripts prepared by myself, David Fisher who was the RADAS editor-in-chief, and others who contributed from time to time became a mine of valuable material for other missionary friends like Joseph Steiner far away in Monaco. Response to the programme was wonderful. Believers were strengthened by their contents, and many unbelievers newly came to put their faith and trust in God because of what they heard. Later it was a joy to meet some of these, even in the most remote regions like Mongolia.

Then, in the early 1990s when the communist governments of central and eastern Europe came to be replaced by more democratic ones, Christian radio stations rapidly sprang up in places for so long as unlikely and as unexpected as Moscow itself. Broadcasting to former communist regions from outside could then be much reduced, releasing much sought after financial resources to help newly liberated and ambitious national churches in countries like Hungary in other valuable ways.

Somewhat curiously, it was not until after our Russian language transmissions of RADAS had ended in 1993 that a fresh wave of invitations for me to give public talks on science/Christian faith topics once more began to multiply in my in-tray. From the occasional talk here and there, I suddenly found myself receiving invitations from a wide range of organisations and places, especially in the UK, Australia and central and eastern Europe.

Increasingly, many of these requests came from Hungary itself, particularly from pastors, church planters and youth leaders. Some were for individual talks, and some for mini-series in specially arranged outreach campaigns.

The first such series was organised by Baptist church planters Jonatón and Örsi in Gyöngyös, a pleasant college town at the western gateway to the Mátra Mountains, and about 80 miles north east of the capital. A programme of talks was arranged in the large Agricultural University. On the first day I was asked to give a 'secular' lecture, on *'The Use of Satellite Data for Crop Monitoring and Harvest Prediction'*, whose purpose was to establish my credentials as a modern scientist. This was followed in the same lecture room after a short break by a second talk of a more Christian nature. I gave this the title: *'Science, the Christian Faith, You and Me'*. I was delighted to find that my interpreter - all the way from Budapest for the occasion - was Ildico. I had already got to know her as one of those Hungarian relatives of Joseph Steiner who could so easily have suffered on account of his bravery and continued faithfulness in sharing the Gospel with his compatriots from TWR, Monte Carlo, as Chapter 1 explained.

We were all excited to find that the audience for the second lecture was actually twice the size of that for the first. However, we were even happier when we learnt the outcome of response forms that members of the audience had been encouraged to fill in before the evening had ended. Jonatón was elated to discover that one quarter of everyone attending the talks had indicated that they now wanted to learn more about God.

Next evening there was an opportunity for some of them to do so. Twenty-five crowded into a small apartment room to hear the third talk: *'Can a scientist be a Christian?'* - a theme requested specifically by Jonatón for that occasion. Then the fun really began! After my one-hour address the less formal question session got under way. It lasted for every minute of three further hours. By the end both I and young Gábor who was interpreting for me were mentally exhausted. But the exchanges had clearly been thought provoking, and positively fruitful for almost everyone.

And now, as I correct my original typescript for this chapter, I can recall an even longer session with a large roomful of responsive students and staff in the University of Veszprém in March 2003. After fully five hours of intensive interaction some of the young people even insisted in quizzing me for another hour in my bedroom in one of the dormitory blocks on campus. At midnight as we closed, the Lord brought several to the prayerful point of deeper personal commitment to Him and His service.

The very next evening the situation I found in the Budapest University of Economic Science and Public Administration was different again. On this occasion it was my happy responsibility to counsel both a Christian student and a teacher of English after a talk attended by about 150 despite competition for an audience from the Hungarian Chancellor of the Exchequer in the next lecture hall. Such was the interest in the science/Christian faith topic that I heard later his audience was the smaller of the two.

Word of the impact of the original presentations in Gyöngyös had spread quickly to the other side of the country. Jonatón often phones his Dad Árpád, an evangelist now based in the old Roman town of Szombathely near the border with Austria. The next Sunday I was booked to give a science/Christian faith message in a specially publicised service of Kőszeg Baptist Church, to be held in a cinema in the town. This is an historic building, noted for its connections with the celebrated Hungarian composer Franz Josef Liszt who gave recitals there. Árpád made a suggestion for that afternoon which would mean I could only arrive in Kőszeg with about ten minutes to spare before my presentation there would be due to begin: "Would Eric first speak in the Szombathely church meeting in the Museum Lecture Theatre in mid-afternoon?"

With some trepidation I said I would add in such a talk. We learned later that in both Kőszeg and Szombathely people came who had never before attended meetings of those two local fellowships. Good contacts were made, which bore fruit in the future.

In Chapter 1 we saw how other similar talks have also by now been given in community centres in villages like that in Recsk, to general village audiences for whom the type of science/Christian faith talk has to be even more 'popular'. The same has been true in schools, whether the audience has been senior pupils to whom talks can be given in English - like those to a third of the students in the private *Református Kollégium* in Pápa - or to younger teens in the Hungarian language as in the state *iskola* in Felscút.

Meanwhile at the other end of the spectrum I have much enjoyed addressing professional scientists of the Christian Prayer Group in the Hungarian Academy of Sciences laboratories in Budapest.

****

What is the flavour of the talks I give? For the village crowd in Recsk I found at the last minute that I had been given the topic:

'*Who or what is watching us from up there?*' Fortunately I was readily able to develop this through reference to my work with Earth observation satellites, before proceeding to remark how, even as a young lad, I had been worried by the Bible assertion that *"You (God) see me, and test my thoughts about You"* (Jeremiah 12:3).

It was then a short step to begin describing my personal route to faith in God, not just as a judge of what I might do wrong, but even more as a loving friend who could help me through all the joys and sorrows, trials and triumphs of life.

As I look back on my conversion experience as a twelve year old boy, it is with interest that I note how similar this was to the 'scientific method' which I have since learned to follow in my professional career. And it is often useful to describe this in the course of my science/Christian faith addresses because it provides the seeking listener with a path to faith that they could follow too.

When I was a lad I was sent by my mother to be a choirboy in a church not far from our home. There was advantage in this for my family: they were able to enjoy a short time without me in the house to raise a din! And there was an advantage for me too, for in that church choirboys were paid. We were not paid much, but coming from a home where every penny had to be watched carefully, my pay for singing in the choir was small but significant. It usually doubled my weekly pocket money. But worship had no meaning for me otherwise.

Suddenly I began to <u>observe</u> changes in the lives of my mother, then my sister, which greatly pleased me because they became kinder to me. But it also greatly puzzled me for the changes were so sharp and sudden. Trying to <u>analyse</u> the reasons why they had changed so much, I concluded it was something to do with another church they had recently begun attending regularly. Out of curiosity one evening I played hookey from the choir and accompanied them to see how this other church was different from mine. To cut another long story short, I found that most other people there were similar in some kind of indeterminate inner way to how my mother and sister had become. They seemed to have something valuable that I did not have, but which I quickly began to covet also.

I never returned to my own church again. Instead I soon came - most unexpectedly - to the point where I knew I had to <u>put to the test</u> myself the insistence of one preacher that if anyone repented of their sins in the sight of God, He would forgive them and grant them a wholly new start in life. Better still, He would also be with them to help them live as He wished, in close fellowship with Him.

I knew I had to respond.

From that point on I saw everything through different eyes: the eyes of faith in God. I had been 'born again'!

Thereafter the call was to apply to my life the knowledge and wisdom which is available through His Word, and to publish such life-changing news so that others would be able to respond to the love of God in their own experiences too. Like every other Christian Believer I have a personal responsibility to share my faith, in the hope that more will want to enjoy the rich blessings of knowing God.

And these five steps - observation, analysis, testing of hypotheses, application of new findings and publication of the results - are ones which every scientist recognises, for they comprise the 'scientific method', the way he or she normally works in the pursuit of any scientific goal.

To more intellectual audiences than the very mixed ones found in Hungarian villages, the styles and contents of my talks are developed along more technical lines. At the end of one such presentation to a hot, packed room of students in a dormitory building in the western suburbs of Budapest in February 2002, I recall a lively debate sparked by comments I had made on some differences between science and the Christian faith.

"Science," I had suggested, "can be defined as: *'Something we do today so that others will be able to do it better tomorrow.'* It's a GROUP activity! We begin our own research where others have led us, ever since our distant ancestors first began trying to understand the way things work. And when we end our investigations, others will take over at that point - or even before we have retired, because as soon as any result or plausible hypothesis is published, the scientific pack is on to it in a flash!"

After a pause for effect, I continued: "But on the other hand, the Christian faith is an INDIVIDUAL thing. It is: *'Something which we all need to engage in today, for none of us can be sure of tomorrow!'* And I should stress, too, that no one else can exercise such faith on our behalf. We have to do this for ourselves - and God will hold us personally accountable for how we respond - or fail to respond - to Him."

Like many such meetings, that crowded one lasted longer than expected. Because of a prior arrangement to leave at a particular time to travel on to my next port of call, I had to leave before some of the students did. Many stayed on for more informal discussions with the organisers. It was already quite late in the evening, and even as it was I would not reach my bed for the night the right side of midnight. Later, though, I heard from 'Dr. Géza', who had been my host there in Budatétény, that the Holy Spirit had been at work that evening. The young man who had shyly told me that he, personally, would soon take the step of faith in Jesus Christ had since done so very positively.

'Dr. Géza' himself is a high-ranking scientist in the prestigious Hungarian Academy of Sciences. One day I accompanied him on his usual journey to work from his Budapest suburban home to his downtown office, a fascinating trip, not by car as might have been expected, but by mainline train, two Metro sectors and a tram.

This was to another 'double header' engagement. First I was expected to give a technical talk to his staff on: *'Satellite remote sensing of crops and crop weather'*, then one to the Academy's Prayer Group on some of those 'modern parables' of which I am so fond. Through them I encouraged the Christians present to search for Scriptural truths in their own areas of research too, for it is so good to see our everyday activities in the contexts of eternity.

On another memorable occasion I was to follow a similar general theme when asked to speak to a large Friday evening congregation in May 2002. This was in Békés near the Rumanian border, and the home church to which Noémi had returned after her two-year stay in Bristol. As I sat on the platform of that big modern building, I glanced over the audience of over 200 that had gathered to hear the 'distinguished English professor' speak. And I smiled as I recalled how my topic had been agreed... off-road in the Orgovány outback of central Hungary one week earlier.

In Orgovány I had been revisiting Károly and Ágnes in their self-built home mission base. As we have seen, their village is one of the most remote in Hungary, well away from main roads in the Danube plain. As we will see in more detail in another context in Chapter 7, outsiders do not go there without specific reason. Thus, much of the life of the village seems unaffected by the Twenty-first Century world. Károly and Ágnes, though, have developed ministries that reach far and wide from Orgovány, indeed to every corner of the Hungarian speaking region. They were delighted with the sample flipchart set Noémi and I were able to give them at that time - the first of many, for the following October I was to leave them nearly 50 sets to distribute on our joint behalf.

Having a morning to spare, Károly took Noémi and me out in his car to see some of the surrounding countryside. Members of his family had farmed there for generations past. It was a fascinating trip, mostly along dirt tracks or even over none, through woods and sand dunes with no landmarks evident to us by which any driver could navigate. In one particularly desolate spot, where we had briefly stopped while Károly told us more of the history of that place, Noémi's mobile phone rang. The pastor of her church was calling. He wanted a title for that talk I was due to give in Békés one week thence. For publicity purposes, could we call him back with the title in no more than <u>ten minutes</u>? This was URGENT!

The next piece of news from Noémi was even worse: "They know you have worked for NASA," she reported, "and want you to talk about that. But you must remember that many of the congregation will be farming people, so you must keep everything simple, and down to earth!"

Now to that point in time I had not given the forthcoming talk in Békés more than a moment's thought. Before it, there were maybe a dozen others I was booked to give... plus many people to meet, discussions to share, and perhaps 1000 miles of travel to negotiate. And all that would be in Noémi's Dad's 30 year old Polish-built Lada car, driven by liquid petroleum gas, and with instruments in the Cyrillic script! No, I had had many other things on my mind.

Now at least in my case, rapid reaction rarely results in real inspiration. Thus, the best suggestion I could concoct on the spur of the moment was: *Modern parables from my work with NASA and other international agencies.* This suggestion was duly relayed by Noémi to her pastor - and I wondered all through the week if the choice of that title had been wise.

When the next Friday came I was immediately encouraged by the excellence of my interpreter, Esztér, whom I had actually met the afternoon following our off-road tour in Orgovány. As a distant relative of Károly and Ágnes she had come, with many others from all over Hungary, to attend a family reunion. An English teacher in the town of Békéscaba near Békés, she lent me confidence and as I was speaking I was also aware of what used to be called 'the liberty of the Spirit'. Is it significant that this expression seems to be used more rarely in the UK today...?

Having been urged to say something about my work with NASA, I did so in opening, and smiled at the frisson that rippled across the audience as I recalled how I had once received a letter from that well-known organisation inviting me to apply for training as an astronaut! And I was amused by the widespread incredulity when I went on to explain how - after the initial feeling of flattery had worn off - I had happily screwed up the letter and tossed it into the nearest waste paper bin in my university office. It was almost as if many in Békés Baptist Church were simultaneously thinking, "How could anyone do THAT! What an opportunity to throw away!"

So I quickly offered my explanation: the invitation had stressed that embarking on such a course of action would require 'complete commitment' to the cause. This is something I know I owe the Lord, but no-one and nothing else, however alluring or glamorous they might sound, deserve such elevated degrees of dedication...

With that attention-assuring opening behind me, I proceeded to outline the old RADAS series of radio transmissions, and the crucial part their compatriot Joseph Steiner had played in helping to bring them about. Knowing that many in my audience grew crops, and constantly struggle with the ravages of insect pests, I explained the point and purposes of modern parables and then described some of my own studies of the desert locust. Drawing from those efforts I had made in Rome for the United Nations agency FAO, I described how, until the 1960s it had been thought that there were two key species, the aptly named 'solitary' and 'gregarious' locusts. The former live in ones or twos scattered thinly across vast areas of desert doing little harm to anything. The latter are company loving, living in swarms that can so easily devastate large areas of crops or natural vegetation.

Then, in a celebrated piece of scientific detective work, two British zoologists - with the very un-British names of Uvarov and Popov - discovered that the two locust types are but different phases of the life cycle of a single species. Given the right environmental conditions, individual solitary locusts can change their colour, shape, size and behaviour to become gregarious.

Dr. George Popov was one of the other consultants with whom I had liaised in Rome and in Algiers at the North African Desert Locust Control Centre. The aim of my work in Algiers was to develop ways of using Earth observation satellite data to help prevent potentially devastating locust plagues from forming unnoticed in the depths of the Saharan and Arabian deserts. If control teams on the ground or in the air were more effectively directed to the locations where egg laying was taking place, then spraying could be more effective too.

And what encourages egg laying to take place?

In one word, RAINFALL!

Run-off after showers dampens the floors of *wadis* and other depressions where the water can accumulate, enabling female locusts to lay their eggs in the softened soil. Plants popping up in the rain freshened ground provide ready breakfast, lunch and tea for hoppers when they hatch out. As in all classic aerial warfare campaigns, the trick is then to hit those immature and flightless insects before they are able to take to the air. In this way the threat to other more cultivated areas can be removed, possible famine averted and even many lives saved.

Now this is an interesting scientific story in its own right, but the question I then posed in Békés was: "How might Jesus, if He were here today, proceed if He had chosen this situation as the basis for a parable?"

Remembering that a parable is: 'an Earthly story with a Heavenly meaning', He might have pressed home His point like this: *"And now I say to you, are not the two locust phases like the two types of people we see in the world? They have different behaviour patterns, keep different company, and even look different from each other. They are those who love the world, and those who love Me...."*

So, you may ask, if it is possible for us, like locusts, to undergo 'personal phase changes', how may they be triggered? Concluding this part of my talk in Békés, I pointed out that this is only possible through an appropriate response to Jesus Christ, the 'living water', the One who said of Himself in John 4:13-14: *"Whoever drinks the water I give him will never thirst. Indeed, the water I give will become in Him a spring of water welling up to eternal life."*

My second modern parable in that talk in Békés involved a situation that had developed at a nuclear power station bear Bristol, for I knew that there were power plants of that type just over the Hungarian border in Rumania. A friend of mine who was a nuclear power engineer had told me how he had been asked to trouble shoot at the station not far from Bristol, for the plant had been under performing.

I therefore entitled this tale the *'Mystery of the missing megawatts'*. The conclusion reached at the end of my friend's investigation had been fascinating: there was no problem with the design of that power station... but this had been compromised by some of the materials used in its construction. This was particularly so in the all-important boiler system, where the nuclear energy is converted into steam to drive the turbines and so generate electricity.

So in this case too, what lesson might the Lord have drawn? Maybe this:

"And now I say to you, many who follow Me are like that under-performing power plant. I have set out in my teaching the perfect blueprint for lives which will honour my Father and well serve your fellow men. But some of the stuff you insist on building into the fabric of your lives is so substandard that you cannot do all the good that you should. This is why so many of you achieve so little for the Kingdom of Heaven."

For my third and final modern parable on that occasion I returned to the universally popular topic of spaceflight with which I had opened my address. I remarked how 'spaceports' are maybe the most exciting places to visit on Earth today, especially when a rocket stands primed and ready on the launch pad. When our children, Andrew and Stella were much younger, we all went to Cape Kennedy in Florida, and toured the world's most famous launch facilities. The official tour included the Mission Control Room, with its familiar banks of monitors arrayed before the huge wall-sized map across which spacecraft orbits are electronically traced.

For me, however, the big surprise was the display on the chief mission controller's screen. Space flight folk lore supposes that, like the audible countdown sequence so familiar to us all, this reads: *'Six... five... four... three... two... one... LAUNCH!'"*

But I saw that, in reality, the master monitor reads: *'Six... five... four... three... commit... ignite... LIFT OFF!'*

"And so I say to you," Jesus living on Earth in the space age might observe, *"the lives of which my Father will be pleased are those that rise like a rocket high above the humdrum of a sinful, fallen world. To reach such heights of glory, people must first commit themselves completely to My cause, for only then can they be fully fired by the flame of the Holy Spirit in their souls. Why is it that so many resist My will, and fear the Spirit's force? Only this can lift men and women to the levels reached by the few, not by the many who feebly and half-heartedly follow Me!"*

I ended my talk in Békés with two challenges. One was for any who had specially heard the voice of God that evening to respond to Him as they knew they should. The other was for everyone to think through at least one modern parable from their own lives and experiences, whether these were from science or not. And I had two principal reasons in mind for making such suggestions. On the one hand conceiving our own parables from modern life can make us more sensitive to the images of God and His dealings with mankind that surround us today, just as they did when Jesus Christ was a man Himself. And on the other hand, such ready made pictures of eternal truths can be useful when we are in conversations with unbelievers, and wish to develop them in a spiritual way....

Some of my own suggestions for modern parables drawn from everyday life now also involve Hungarian history, geography, and even the Hungarian kitchen. One involves the mythical Turul Bird. Carvings or images of this are evident all over Hungary, from the one hundred foot high statue on the steep cliffs of Buda in the nation's capital to miniature motifs on clothing, ties, tablecloths and the like. But ask a young Hungarian how and why the Turul Bird legend was born and most have no idea at all. Sadly, the Cross of Jesus Christ is a similarly familiar symbol in the modern world, but also one which few young people in Hungary - or the UK are able to explain. Recent polls have further shown that Easter therefore has little or no meaning for large sections of our community.

There is a massive need for those of us who understand the place of the Cross at the very heart of the Christian Gospel to share this with the world. We need to take every possible opportunity to explain how through this Cross it is possible to find God personally, and come to enjoy being at peace with Him.

Thus today there is a wide range of addresses I can offer when asked to speak on a science/Christian faith theme. More are being developed all the time. Also, though titles chosen for particular venues may be ones I have used before, each individual talk is tailored carefully to the new place and likely audience expected for it. Changes in style and content are sometimes even necessary once I have seen an audience, and the presentation has begun.

When any series of talks is requested, as for Jászberény in late February 2002, careful planning is put into the programme in my home as well as in the town itself. Hungarian friends like Noémi while she was in Bristol, Peter and Zsuzsa in nearby Keynsham, and Tamás far away in Jászberény help with translations of the lecture summaries I put on overhead transparencies, along with captions for key pictures and graphics. These help ensure that those who will attend can focus both audibly and visually on the chosen themes.

Friends sometimes ask: "Isn't it cumbersome to lecture through interpreters?" My answer to this is: "No, because the thinking time that interpretation gives between each sentence helps the speaker to be more concise and less repetitive than is usually the case with a single language presentation. Also, I think it is good if people hear the Gospel in their own language, from one of their own compatriots. But I always insist on running through my talks with the interpreter before a talk, so that we can plan the best translations for terms and concepts he or she may not have encountered before. We also discuss the most effective ways to convey key spiritual truths to mindsets which can be different from ours."

This, then is a growing and developing ministry that I have come to enjoy, despite all my original and long-standing misgivings. It is certainly a ministry appreciated by Hungarian church leaders. One of them actually urged: "Give up the building team work you do, and spend more of your time giving these talks for us! We'll help organise them for you. Just tell us whenever you're available, and how you would like things done. It will then be our privilege to help set them up!"

As always, though, the Holy Spirit has to have the final say. When I sent exploratory letters to three or four places in the winter of 2001/2002 I was mystified to receive a particularly strong response from Jászberény, a town which at that time I had never visited. I had previously met Tamás, the pastor's assistant at the Jászberény Bible Baptist Church elsewhere, and his name and address were in our email directory. I had not intended to send him one of those letters of enquiry - but by mistake(?) he received one anyway, responded to it very positively, and the campaign in his town was a model of its kind. Despite the cold, frosty nights that February, good audiences gathered for the three talks in the Teacher's College, and the Holy Spirit blessed them all.

One such source of blessing was of a particularly unexpected kind. In arranging the events, the ten year old Bible Baptist Church in the town had joined forces with the three hundred year old Lutheran Church, the first time the two congregations had co-operated in any way. "We're so happy you came," remarked several people afterwards, "because it has helped us Christians from different Fellowships get to know one another. We're sure this will be the beginning of a real partnership in the work of the Gospel in this district!" Just as significantly, since the campaign, new personal contacts have been followed up. New spiritual fruit has also resulted among some who were Believers when the talks were staged.

Thinking further back, I recall how the RADAS programmes I had helped prepare between 1980 and 1993 had been directed both towards existing members of the churches in communist countries and folk who were still searching for the meaning and purpose of life. In different ways and different places the same kinds of materials and arguments I developed first for radio are still being used of the Lord today, both to strengthen His Church and to point seekers to the Saviour.

My thinking has come a long way since soft-spoken Joseph Steiner first challenged me to cross that high personal hurdle I had not wanted even to approach. But I am glad that with God's help it was finally faced and surmounted, so that much of my special secular knowledge and training can still be used and blessed by the Him. Whether this may be to a clutch of Christian professional scientists, as in the Hungarian Academy of Sciences in June 2002, or a crowd of ordinary townsfolk in Bicske's Cultural Centre in January 2003, or one third of the student body of Pápa's *Református Kollégium* in March 2003, I count each opportunity to explore the handiwork of God in the universe and His personal concern for mere mortals like us an enormous privilege. Each is a fresh chance to share the Gospel and to enthuse fellow Believers more concerning His special love for His redeemed children everywhere.

And is it not the most natural thing that every one of us who knows the Lord personally should be able to serve Him most specifically through our own individual areas of life and experience? With His help we can ALL successfully cross much higher hurdles than we could ever do alone.

CHAPTER 7

HIDDEN TREASURE

Home of the Good News Foundation

Some countries - like England - have a hectic heartland. Aptly, the English Midlands have been called the 'engine room of the nation'. But some other countries - like Australia - have remote, even mysterious centres, parts of which are rarely visited by outsiders even after the advent of airways and motorways. Surprising though it may seem, Hungary is more like the latter than the former. Just as Australia's capital, Canberra, is nearer the edge than the middle, so too is Hungary's, Budapest. Furthermore, wide regions of central Hungary are known only to people with real cause to visit them.

Despite such unexpected similarities between Australia and Hungary there are also some significant differences. One is that the centre of the southern continent is desiccated desert, whereas the heart of Hungary is the floodplain of one of Europe's greatest waterways, the dominating Danube. And while there is little precipitation in the Australian Outback, the Danube plain can be the scene of both heavy snowfalls in winter and spectacular thunderstorms in summer. So I have contrasting recollections of the middles of these two nations. One indelible memory I have of Alice Springs is of the dry riverbed where an annual regatta is held. In most years the bed is so dry that the crews have to pick up their boats and run with them! Conversely, I shall never forget the April I was visiting central Hungary, and witnessed floods one day, and deep snow the next.

In Chapter 6 we saw in passing what an out-of-the-way place the village of Orgovány is, even though near to the geographic centre of the nation. Yet, on the Christian map of that country it is truly one of the principal points. The chief reason for this is one remarkable family, headed by our old friends Károly and Ágnes, the parents of Pálma whom we met in Chapter 1. But before seeing more of what they do for the Lord, it is worth painting a more detailed picture of the place where they live.

Orgovány is one of the many *Nagyalföld* settlements where, even at the beginning of the Twenty-first Century, cars still seem no more plentiful than horse-drawn carts. It is also one of the few areas of the country where the almost legendary *csettegő*, a remarkable little petrol driven vehicle virtually unique to Hungary. can still be encountered frequently, chugging along with the noise that has inspired its manufactured name: *CHET-ee-goh... CHET-ee-goh... CHET-ee-go!* These amazing mechanical oddities were specially designed to be classified differently from the tractors they often replaced under the communist collective farm system. Having a small external engine instead of a bigger, internal one, they have never needed licence plates, road tax discs or insurance, despite their frequent use of public roads.

Today the village of Orgovány still boasts little more than a few dirt lanes at right angles to the single main street, plus three or four assorted churches, a junior school and a small handful of shops. Its lone cinema closed some years ago. The smaller of its two restaurants did so very recently. This was an engaging, though diminutive place whose eating area was only big enough for four picnic-style tables with bench-type seats - and then only if one table blocked the door to the kitchen. All the food had to be taken out of the back door of the kitchen, then in again through the front door of the dining room in order to be delivered to the tables.

One or two of the 'main' roads linking Orgovány with the outside world are now metalled, but others are still unsealed. All the access roads or lanes are flanked by drainage ditches. In the absence of streetlights these can be unpleasant traps for the unwary, whether pedestrians or careless car drivers at night. Many of the cottages are of the old traditional 'long house' type, with family accommodation at the road end, declining into livestock sheds and pens towards the other. Finally they peter out in a welter of stores and woodpiles.

Some of the humble homes even retain their original thatched roofs, often very run down and moth eaten in appearance. However, because all the older buildings except the slightly grander of the churches are made of local materials - mostly mud and straw - many of those venerable buildings are now falling down. Newer houses are more durably constructed of breeze blocks, or large, typically east European *ytong* cavity bricks, but Orgovány is still one of the poorer districts in a country which no-one would describe as rich.

Meanwhile, the property Károly and Ágnes own in the middle of the village is one of the newer and smarter ones, owing everything to Károly's building skills and Ágnes's love of flowers and shrubs. Trained as an engineer, Károly felt called to leave that profession in the 1980s to manage a care home for the elderly. At the same time he continued to serve the Lord in a number of other ways too some of which were alluded to in Pálma's poem at the end of Chapter 1. Then, when democracy and freedom were restored in the early 1990s, the family moved back to Orgovány with a new vision, and a lively new hope. Their prayer was that they might make a telling contribution to God's work not only in that place itself, but also from it to many others through their newly established *Alapítvány*, the Good News Foundation.

Locally, there was immediately much for them to do. At the time there was no bright spiritual witness in the village, so the Good News Fellowship was begun in their own home. And there were certainly many folk in need of practical help in the vicinity, not least as agriculture became a more perilous pursuit after COMECON's collapse once communist rule had come to an end. Because the surrounding region has long been a relatively depressed part of Hungary it has fewer gypsies than in the population as a whole. However, as elsewhere in central and eastern Europe this significant minority presents special challenges all its own. Little by little Károly and his family extended their home to embrace a larger church room and accommodation for visitors of different kinds, plus storage space for the clothing, footwear, bedding and food which began to arrive in considerable quantities from the West. Much of this has been distributed among the gypsy community.

A garage was required, too, for the 'SGA car' which is stationed in Orgovány. When British SGA field staff need this for onward travel into other countries of Eastern Europe, Károly meets them at

Budapest Airport, and off they go. The rest of the year the vehicle is at the disposal of Károly and Ágnes, and does sterling service in the Orgovány neighbourhood.

Today the whole *Örömhír Alapítvány* development is a smart and wonderfully God-honouring complex. When Noémi of flipchart fame arrived there with her father's Lada towards the end of May 2002 to partner me on my long journey around half the country, her reaction to the home base of the Good News Foundation was a spontaneous: "Isn't this <u>beautiful!</u>" Indeed, whether it had been late spring with its flowers and fresh green tree foliage, or any other part of the year, hers would have been a most appropriate remark.

And the compound is still growing. Károly walked us through a gateway in the high stone wall into the courtyard of the next property. This is owned by Károly's elderly mother. Parts of it are now in use for young people's activities. Károly then told us the recent story of the next block after that, at the junction of their dirt lane and another. He related how the empty plot had belonged to a Christian lady, but he had begun to hope that his Fellowship might be able to acquire it for a larger church and store, as well as a children's playground. The plans for the central, two-storey building sat ready waiting on his home computer.

Károly, knowing there were no funds to purchase the land, in faith approached the owner. He asked if she would consider selling it to the Foundation. She said she needed time to think about that.

"After a few weeks," Károly recalled with a happy smile, "she came back to me and said: 'No, I can't <u>sell</u> it to you… but I will GIVE it to you, because I am sure this is what the Lord wants me to do!'"

Part of the patch has already been equipped with swings and roundabouts for the children. Another part is marked out with pegs awaiting resources with which the foundations of the new church and storehouse can be lain. Truly this is a space well worth watching in the future.

Ministries to gypsies

Among those from the village who come to Károly and Ágnes's centre in the course of an average week are several gypsy children. We have seen that this distinctive ethnic group is widely spread over central and eastern Europe. It is also everywhere disliked. In Hungary alone there are about three-quarters of a million gypsies, making up about one in fourteen of the population. Their skins are somewhat darker than those of their few true British cousins, but their general habits are very similar. By nature the Romanys are wanderers, loath to settle, and even harder to absorb into 'normal' life styles and communities. Their own cultural heritage and traditions are quite different from those of the more settled societies among which they move, and some of their habits are both hard to understand and even harder to accept by more average mortals.

On the other hand, in certain contexts gypsies undeniably add colour and romance to the local scene. For example, I well remember my first encounter with gypsy musicians, on my first ever visit to Hungary in the mid-1960s. On some balmy evenings a number of us from the Summer School at Debrecen University would enjoy an *al fresco* meal in one of the parks near the centre of town. Vivid and exciting music was provided by several Romanies on their fiddles and *csimbalons* - horizontal instruments rather like xylophones, but with strings instead of keys, and which are played with gusto with little padded hammers.

And some Hungarian gypsies, especially Christians, have been among the most generous and hospitable people I have ever met. Győrgy, Márta and their family of six assorted children were like that. Gillian and I were taken to visit them in their home, the Hungarian equivalent of a council house on the edge of Enese, a down-at-heel village 20 miles or so from Győr. The house was cold and damp, and in urgent need of decoration and repair. It was furnished in a sparse and scrappy way. Then, when Márta went to get some milk for the tea she was making for us, I caught a glimpse of the inside of the large upright refrigerator in their kitchen-cum-dining-room. Whereas at home in the UK most freezers are full of food and drink, this one was almost completely bare.

Győrgy was sitting by the kitchen table with one leg in plaster, from the hip down to the foot. Employed as an iron foundryman, his leg had been badly broken when a crucible of molten metal had swung out of control and collided with him fair and square. Insurance for the workers in his factory was very basic, and following the collapse of communism the welfare system was in a state of ruin. Thus, the weekly income in his household was minimal. Without help from their church, the family would have been in even direr straits than we could see they were. In such circumstances, would we have placed a great plateful of home made doughnuts on the table for our visitors… and insisted when they left that they must take the whole new packet of English Breakfast Tea, obviously bought specially to satisfy their guests' exotic taste…?

Christian Gypsies in Orgovány and neighbouring villages fit the György and Márta pattern too. It is principally to help such disadvantaged people that Károly and Ágnes have constructed their aid store. Periodically this is replenished with truckloads of useful goods delivered by the Blythswood organisation operating out of Glasgow, and more occasionally by other western European charities. The SGA car has been a vital means of ferrying items discarded by the likes of us out to the gypsy families, and other hard-up folk across that remote and impoverished stretch of central Hungary.

Usually the things delivered from the West are wholly useful, and much appreciated. Just occasionally though, some items underline the need for more careful and critical thought by distant donors. On one of our early visits to Orgovány, Károly showed us a stack of dozens of heavy, three-litre cans of liquid that had recently arrived as part of one truck load of aid. Unfortunately the cans were all labelled, identically, in French. Károly asked me if I could decipher what the contents were. However, my old GCE 'O' level ability in that language is nowadays rusty with infrequent use. It got us some way with the translation of the labels, but no further. There were a few key words that I simply did not recognise. Returning home, we invited a friendly French teacher to help with them. She explained a little later that the cans contained a special fluid for the relief of nursing mothers who were suffering from sore, cracked nipples!

Presumably this was surplus stock from some major hospital, or a supplier who had over estimated demand in the British Isles. But enough of the stuff had been sent to Orgovány to treat most of the mothers with babies over the whole of Hungary! Worse still, it was also already out of date, and we rued the space and weight it had wasted on the delivery vehicle all the way from the UK. The story is worth relating here both to stress that it is expensive to move heavy goods so far across the continent, and to underline that sending aid anywhere should not be seen just as a convenient way of ridding ourselves of things we no longer need.

Meanwhile, the love, sympathy and understanding shown to gypsies of all ages by Károly, Ágnes and their son and daughter, Donát and Lilla who still live at home, is in a different league from that generally accorded them. The gypsy children particularly enjoy the homework classes and games evenings that punctuate the week between Sunday services and Friday Bible Circles. It is specially touching to see swarthy, black-haired, dark-eyed gypsy kids in happy huddles around blonde, blue eyed Lilla, a teacher by profession but more importantly a warm-hearted Believer who so naturally spreads the love of the Lord even to folk whom most other Hungarians treat as unlovable.

Home of the Good News Fellowship

The present church room is on the ground floor of the cluster of buildings Károly has designed and largely built himself with the aid of his family. It is a homely sanctuary. Its partly pine-panelled walls are enlivened with colourful scenic posters complete with Scripture texts. As in many evangelical churches in Hungary the focal wall behind the lectern is plain white, embellished with a simple wooden cross. In one corner of the room we find the frequent modern substitutes for the church organ of earlier generations - a keyboard, some electric guitars, a set of drums and a microphone for the worship leader, usually Lilla. Coils of black cable snake across the dais floor.

The seating for the congregation is particularly commonplace. As in many growing Hungarian churches it consists of white plastic patio chairs. To us at first these may seem incongruous in such a context. I have even heard some Western friends remark disapprovingly: "Surely there are <u>more appropriate</u> chairs for churches?"

"Yes," I have answered, "but when you hear Hungarian pastors exclaim: 'Our members have learnt what it means to '<u>give until it hurts</u>' to buy even these, you will appreciate that the plastic chairs they buy at maybe £3 each are the best they can afford. The £10 upholstered chairs I bought for the church at Komárom with Gillian's KLM ticket money are usually way out of reach of most churches outside Budapest. And remember, too, that seven-month pregnant Joli didn't have even one spare £3 plastic chair to sit on in her kitchen...!"

Yet despite the plastic chairs, Sunday worship in the Good News Fellowship in Orgovány is very lively, and 'The Word' received attentively. As in so many of the Bible-believing churches in the Hungarian world an open prayer session often immediately follows the preaching of that Word. Maybe this is one reason why new converts seem to grow so quickly in their fresh faith, for 'hearing' is routinely followed by audible 'responding', and then by 'doing'. The personal reflection and response that such prayer times promote are active links between the message from the pulpit and the person in the pew.

Meanwhile, the prayer meetings themselves, each Friday evening are full of prayer. Not with those Christians do we find the 'no prayer' or maybe 'one prayer' syndromes often encountered in the UK.

And as for long silences, in gatherings like those in Orgovány, they are unknown.

Personal and public ministries, near and far

In addition to the pastoral leadership that Károly and Ágnes afford the church in their home, they also exercise some rare and special ministries in and from their quiet and centrally located base in the very heart of Hungary. One of these specialised services is personal and private, the other much more public, helping whole fellowships rather than individuals in them.

That special private ministry, undertaken unobtrusively yet at considerable cost to the family, at least in time spent on it, is in personal counselling. In this they have been so greatly used of God that people come to them from far and wide in search of help. The value of the help they give, measured by such priceless things as renewed faith in God, refreshed ministries and restored personal relationships is incalculable. It is all the more important too, because of the well-known and historically attested Hungarian fascination with suicide, which therefore claims more victims here per head of the population than elsewhere across most of the rest of Europe.

Károly recalls one man who came to see him and Ágnes while on weekend release from hospital where he had been on and off for years as a foil to suicidal fits of depression. After intensive counselling from the Word of God he went home declaring he was much better already. Soon afterwards his wife phoned to say he had begun working again, as a joiner. Within a few months the news was better still: he was doing so well that he had been promoted to supervise ten workers in his firm.

The latest word to Károly and Ágnes from that man is that: "Life is wonderful!"

His wife agrees: "He's VERY well," she says happily, "and is now in charge of 40 others. We praise God for His goodness to us - and for the help you both gave him at such a crucial time!"

And Ágnes remembers the 21-year old young woman who came to stay with them a couple of years ago from the nearby city of Kecskemét. A little earlier Károly and Ágnes had been visiting the girl's family. All of a sudden her father had exclaimed: "Our daughter is suffering from clinical depression!"

The man's wife had tried to hush him up, embarrassed that others might learn their unhappy family secret. Yet it was too late: the truth was out - but Károly and Ágnes promised to do all they could to help.

As things transpired they had to do a lot, for the girl came to stay in Orgovány for three whole weeks, receiving counselling every evening and sometimes in the mornings too. At first she insisted that: "I'm sure the Lord will never be able to forgive me!" However, she began to respond to the steady warmth of His love, and the care shown by Károly and Ágnes. Before the third week had ended she was taken - now unwillingly! - by her parents to a prearranged consultation with a psychiatrist. During it, she surprised the doctor, by gladly enjoining that she was no longer taking the medication he had previously prescribed for her.

"For you see," she exalted, "I HAVE BEEN HEALED BY JESUS CHRIST!"

And time proved her right.

Clinical depression can be a very nasty illness. In some cases recovery may take years. But when the Great Physician Himself becomes involved, as through Károly and Ágnes's essentially private ministry, personal relief and even total healing are much more quickly possible.

And meanwhile, what of that other, very public, ministry that they exercise from their self-built centre? One of the most unexpected sights in such an old-fashioned village, far from the mainstream of Hungarian life, is the interior of a long room in the middle of their property. This is fitted with floor-to-ceiling shelving on all four walls, packed with books, cassettes and videos. On the desk top at one side is one of their computer workstations, plus printers and a fax machine. This is the nerve centre and storeroom of the Good News Foundation, whence spiritual resource materials for all ages and stages of life are despatched to well over one hundred Fellowships and many individuals across the whole of pre-Trianon Hungary.

For us it has been so helpful to be able to distribute the Flipchart Books through Károly and Ágnes's organisation.

Then, in October 2002 we drew up together a broader scheme for the preparation and distribution of a wide range of new Hungarian language devotional books and resource materials to be distributed freely across the whole of the Hungarian-speaking world.

The new plan includes two items conceived in the middle of 2002 by Gillian's bedside, when she was already sleeping most of the time. One is the new concept series of *Bible Story Picture Packs* of which more will be said in Chapter 8. The other involves *Timelines for Teens*, which will take a broad-brush approach to Biblical and post-Biblical history for more senior young people. By seeking to put well known episodes from Scripture into their wider contexts they will show how lessons from them are still personally relevant in the modern day and age.

The Good News Foundation, then and now

But for the time being you may well say: "You have not told us yet how the Good News Foundation come into being. What led Károly - that mechanical engineer turned nursing home manager - to step out in faith with his wife and five children to set up a new type of Christian ministry in the early days of post-communist eastern Europe?" For from that initial leap a work has grown that now helps feed and clothe many people, and help them spiritually, in all five of those countries where Hungarians are specially numerous today.

From 1983 until 1991 Károly, his wife and family lived in the small country town of Kiskőrös, some 15 miles south west of Orgovány, and even nearer the dawdling Danube as it winds its southerly way across central Hungary towards the border with Serbia. Károly and Ágnes loved their ministry among the old people in the Home they managed together and helped maintain. But the politically prompted changes that began to accelerate after the mid-1980s set them thinking increasingly of the fresh opportunities that were arising to address some long-standing spiritual needs.

Károly himself explains:

"In the 'Old Days' no-one was allowed to spread the Gospel. The pastors could talk about it, but only inside a church building or *imaház*. Then from the middle 1980s the system a little bit melted, and gave chances of evangelisation. In 1988 the pastor of the big church in Kiskőrös was able to organise a Children's Camp, the first for many years. He asked Ágnes to do this for about 100 children, because he knew of her gifts. We were so busy with the Home that she said 'No!' - but the pastor came back and said: 'It's your responsibility! If you don't, then WE WON'T...!'

"We knew then it would be sinful to say no, so we said: 'Yes, alright'! It was the right decision. That year and the next many children were converted. Most of them are really committed to the Lord today. Some are pastors, and others leaders in their churches.

"So God began to give us a new calling, to reach out not only to older people, but of all generations. I love old people, but after much praying, and seeing the changes in the government which made witness so much easier, in 1991 we resigned and sold our home to begin this new work, the Good News Foundation. It had taken us three years discussing it with God. We would lose our salaries, and my pension would be small, but He insisted: 'Just depend on Me'! So we did that, for food, clothing, for each other's needs, and those of the whole family. God promised too that others would join us in the new work. We see now that He has been very faithful in everything.

"Today we have volunteer associate workers in over one hundred churches all across Hungary, and in Slovakia, Ukraine, western Rumania and Vojvodina. The associate workers have a range of functions. Many collect clothing and food, and distribute these things to needy people, especially Christian families in their own areas. About twice a year we get a truckload of aid from Blythswood in the UK, and this is good because most used clothing and shoes we collect in Hungary is very much worn. Our unmarried son and daughter Donát and Lilla also help us much.

"Others of our workers have different tasks. Some prepare cassettes and books to be lent out. Some look after mini-libraries and video collections. These include the set of cassettes of the New Testament recorded by Steiner Joseph. Others contain preaching and teaching by national Christians, or by famous English or American pastors, with Hungarian voice-overs. You see, many people in our country and its next door neighbours can't afford to BUY books, videos or cassettes, but are glad to be able to borrow them. This way we can encourage Believers to learn more of the Lord, and share Him with unbelievers too.

"We also have a little devotional magazine - like the one you saw me give the lady in the TESCO 'Bureau de Change' in Kecskemét today. That issue had reports of a Retreat we held in the summer, and letters from people saying what it had meant for them. They explained how God had really touched their lives.

"The Flipchart Books you are providing for us to distribute are wonderful. It is good we can give them free of charge, for many churches could never afford to buy things like that. We also look forward to receiving the *Bible Story Picture Packs* and *Timelines for Teens* as soon as they are ready. We thank all the British Christians who in IN ANY WAY are helping make these possible."

Heavenly treasure is for sharing

Very recently, unexpected help from British Christians has also brought *Hidden Treasure*, another of Károly's projects, to full fruition. Like other countries of central and eastern Europe, around 1990 Hungary turned the corner onto the road towards a more democratic, free market future. This has released a great wave of demand for more Christian literature than had been available for half a century or more. Home grown Bible based writing has been in particularly short supply. In all those countries Bibles and Scripture portions have been the top priority, and in more up-to-date translations than previously available. Next, concordances, reference books and hymn books have been needed, more or less in that order of priority. Children's materials - especially for group use - have been way down the list. For me one important task is identifying a manageable list of high priorities for which sponsorship might be forthcoming. And remember, through the last few years Hungarian has been one of the most neglected countries in competition for support from the West.

We have amply seen how Károly and Ágnes are people of many parts. Ágnes has further shown her own mettle by preparing some intriguing Bible-based games for children, while Károly has been writing devotional texts. At the outset of 2003 the first of these is now being printed in Hungarian in book form - made possible by a sequence of events which none of us envisaged twelve months before. Together they make up another divinely planned 'coincidence', a happy outcome of an otherwise sad story. This involved the discovery of Gillian's brain tumour in February 2002, followed by surgery, radiotherapy, and then the slow, debilitating decline until her Homecall in September, just two weeks after our Coral wedding anniversary. This was sad for me and the rest of Gillian's family and friends, but so happy for her as she became able to worship face to face the Lord she loved so very much.

When mailing out the letters of invitation to her Thanksgiving Service I wrote that the family would be privileged to provide the flowers, and suggested that any other gifts in her memory could be put towards the printing of 1000 copies of *Hidden Treasure*. Indeed, six months previously I had worked out the cost for these, and promised Károly that Gillian and I would sponsor them - even though we did not know at the time where we would find the money. The day before I travelled back to Hungary in October 2002 for my first visit since Gillian's Homecall, I spoke in her place at a ladies' meeting in Hanham, Bristol. At the end of it an old friend of Gillian's slipped me an envelope. I did not have time to open this before I found myself in Orgovány the following Friday.

I then discovered that it contained a substantial sum - enough to take the total in lieu of flowers to precisely the total I had previously promised Károly and Ágnes four months earlier! Thus it was with special thanksgiving to God that we drew up the following inscription to insert in that new book of Karoly's, and of which Gillian had shown her complete approval:

"Printing of this book has been made possible with gifts from British Christians in memory of Mrs. Gillian M. Barrett, who was called Home into the visible presence of her Saviour and Lord on 30 September 2002: she loved the Hungarian people, and knew much of the power of prayer in her own life."

For me, the way in which the Lord has provided for that book to be published came as a real encouragement at a very testing time. God was already beginning to honour His matchless promise in Romans 8:28, one on which I have come to rely so very much: *"And we know that ALL THINGS work together for the good of those who love Him, who have been called according to His purpose...."*

And I am absolutely sure that it will not be the last such sign. For a start, the publication of that book on prayer will itself multiply the blessing to many more.

Let's summarise

Yes, Orgovány is insignificant on the atlas map of Hungary. But more than a fair share of the treasure of the Kingdom of Heaven on Earth is in that field. It is bringing much joy and benefit to many who love its Giver - whether they live locally or, by reason of the vision and faithfulness of some of God's very special witnesses - almost anywhere across the whole of that wide region where Hungarian is still the first language of the population.

CHAPTER 8

THE CIRCLE WIDENS

From the time Gillian and I came home so thoughtfully from our visit to Hungary in 1995, determined to help the Children's Home in Kőszeg, we knew that there was comparatively little we could do to assist in that country alone. How much more we could do if we could enthuse and involve others too!

By describing some of the ways others have come to help, this chapter is a tribute to all those who have already lent a hand in any one of a multitude of different ways - and to those who have lent two hands, by putting them together in prayer. Some of these friends will be named, but most will not. Indeed, there are many particularly in south west England and South Wales who have contributed in one way or another whom we ourselves have never met. Many of these have even wished to remain anonymous.

The key point is that any 'mission' is pyramidal in shape. The few at the 'sharp end' are supported and supplied by many more at the 'blunt end'. Without their help, efforts like those of *'4H'* to help the Church in Hungary would be extremely slight. Thus, one of the chief purposes of this passage is to recognise and thank those who are helping make so much possible in the Hungarian world today.

Another purpose of this chapter is to prompt others to think: "I wonder if I could go there and be useful too," or: "I wonder if this thing I own, or could get and give, would be more useful to the Lord in Hungary than I think it might be here? In the past, other countries and situations have held my attention, but times change, and I now feel led to help the relatively forgotten Hungarian people as they try to make faster progress for Him."

We noted earlier how members of many Women's Institutes all over Devon helped collect toothbrushes and other toiletries once that epic initial delivery by the big 'Luton-bodied' Transit van in April 1996 had been so greatly appreciated. The van itself, which proved just the right size for that 2500-mile round trip, was kindly loaned and insured at no cost to us by Martyn. He is a good friend from our own church in Bristol who, seven years on, is helping in fresh ways, including providing introductions to Hungarian Christians newly living in this area. Some such folk have already helped us a lot, including Peter and Zsuzsa from nearby Keynsham. As we have already seen, Peter has undertaken several urgent translation tasks, especially when I have been preparing titles and captions for overhead transparencies to use in outreach talks on science and the Christian faith. It is so helpful to be able to project these in Hungarian, thereby lessening some of the problems of instantaneous interpretation. Zsusza has checked scripts for us too.

****

On every one of our Practical Missions to help improve the fabric of church buildings and pastor's accommodation, overland support vehicles have been used to transport some Team members out from the UK, and to carry gifts, tools and locally unavailable materials. These vehicles are even important in Hungary, because they are also used to ferry us from the building sites to our living quarters every day, and to services in other towns or villages. On most occasions we have been lent minibuses by our own church or one in Clevedon, though when our smaller Team went to Kőszeg in the spring of 1999 we were glad to be offered the loan of Stuart and Margaret's privately owned people carrier, as mentioned in Chapter 4.

Several times work has had to be done on the vehicles to prepare them for such long trips, including the fitting or refitting of a tachograph. Such a 'spy in the cab' is required by European Union law for all vehicles to be used on the continent with ten seats or more. Roof racks or roof boxes to increase the carrying capacity are other extras we have usually needed for our vans.

Exactly how Gillian and I came by our tachograph - which is now *'4H'* property - is another inspiring example of how the Lord knows the needs of His people, and can meet them in the most amazing ways. Truly He is: *"...able to do immeasurably more than all we ask or imagine..."* (Ephesians 3:20). Some 20 years ago we befriended two young trainee nurses who had recently begun their courses in Bristol. Soon Gillian introduced Rachel to Steve, one of the eligible young men in our church. Eventually this led to an engagement, marriage, children - and a call to the foreign mission field. Steve, a gifted motor mechanic, had already become involved in Hoveraid, which organised very high profile expeditions to far-flung places including Papua New Guinea and the source of the Yangtse River, high up on the borders of China and Tibet. Steve's task was to keep those exotic machines on the go in some of the most testing conditions in the world.

A year or two later, and just before Steve and Rachel were accepted for full time missionary service with the Unevangelised Fields Mission in the Central Highlands region of Papua New Guinea where Steve would serve as a base maintenance manager, he offered to come with us to Hungary as a member of our Second Practical Team. Because we had commercially rented a minibus for our First Team trip, that was the first on which we planned to use our own church minibus. For it we would need a tachograph of our own. Where would we find one? And how could we get it fitted? Garages were quoting around £2000 for a new tachograph. Even if fitted and fully calibrated, that kind of cost appalled us. We, along with many others prayed, and waited to see if the Lord would somehow intervene....

A mere couple of weeks before the Second Practical Mission was due to commence, Rachel had been asked if she would help cook for a house party from a London church they knew. Steve and the children went to keep her company at the venue in South Wales, hoping for something of a vacation. Events conspired to ensure that, for Steve at least, it would be at best a (mini) busman's holiday!

Almost as soon as they arrived, Steve was told that the van from London had broken down in a major way. The inevitable request to Steve was: "Could you have a look at it for us, please?"

He did, and after a couple of days and a lot of effort the problem was deemed to have been fixed.

The south London church leaders were naturally very grateful to Steve for this, as well as to good cook Rachel. Steve told us later that this encouraged him to be inquisitive: "The minibus was fitted with a tachograph, but had no GB plates, so could not have been outside the British Isles. I mentioned this to their boss, and how we needed a tachograph for Hungary. 'Ours was already fitted when we bought the bus,' came his reply. 'We've never needed it, though, because we don't take the van abroad, and have no intention of doing so. If you can remove it, you can HAVE it! That would be one way we could thank you and Rachel for all you have done for us this week.'

"And so," Steve concluded triumphantly, pulling a dial, some cabling and a black box from his sports bag, "HERE IT IS! I'll fit it to our own church minibus in a day or two. It won't take long."

And that is how the Lord provided that expensive item, fitted, at zero cost to us. We still own and use it to this day - though whenever necessary transferring it to other vehicles.

Since then, specialist help from people like Steve has also been forthcoming on an increasingly wide range of different occasions, and by no means only in relation to Practical Missions. Furthermore, it has been a privilege to arrange for others to help more independently in Hungary, in respect of both 'practical' and 'spiritual' activities. The following few instances must suffice to illustrate these. For convenience, they all involve one local church in Hungary, and are arranged chronologically.

****

Today I still find the call of God to Pastor Lajos and his young wife Mariann as challenging as I did when I first heard of it in 1998. Unusually for a Hungarian pastor, Lajos had received a small honorarium for his previous work, as assistant pastor in a lively church in the relatively affluent lake resort town of Velence. Small, wiry, black-bearded and bright-eyed Lajos - from the moment I met him - struck me as a visionary and a thinker. I soon discovered that he is a mover and a shaker too.

The God we serve often acts as a mover and shaker Himself, and had clearly called Lajos and Mariann to begin planting that new church, and to begin at once. That they obeyed is an object lesson in obedience, for they moved to Bicske in February 1999 just six weeks before their first baby was due to be born. We met them at that time, and it seemed not to concern them that the move would leave them very short of family finance. In Bicske they began meetings with just one old couple in their cottage, and trusted the Lord to supply their urgent - and soon to be increased - personal needs.

Shortly after their initial great leap of faith God gave Lajos and Mariann a little baby boy whom, because of their Jewish ethnic background, they called Manasse. Immediately he intensified their time of testing, for he was born with a ruptured diaphragm. This was a serious genetic defect, and so much so that nurses in the hospital took Polaroid pictures of him when just one day old. It was thought likely he would not survive. Only one surgeon in Hungary is qualified to operate on that condition - and he was to take two goes before Manasse was clearly on the road to recovery. This, though, was a turning point in the family's immediate fortunes. Shortly afterwards SGA stepped in to help support the family and, against its normal practice for church planters more than two years down the line, continued to do so to the time of writing.

However, this is an investment which has been richly rewarded. The new church at Bicske has grown rapidly from the tiny beginnings described above and in Chapter 4. Already today it is very active locally, nationally and even internationally.

In the spring of 2001 the pastor's own family grew further too, with the arrival of twin girls, Priscilla and Anna-Abija. Once more there was a post-natal scare, for Anna-Abija had difficulty breathing, and it was feared that she might be suffering the same problem Manasse had had. Fortunately, her trouble was no more serious than a respiratory infection contracted during the birth process, and after a few days in an oxygen tent Anna-Abija was fine.

Meanwhile, Mariann had been quite ill throughout the pregnancy, which had been taxing for a small person carrying twins. However would she manage with three little people to care for, instead of one?

This is where another different kind of 'specialist' stepped in to help. John, who for so long was the gracious, hard working caretaker of our Bristol church, was called Home to Heaven in May 2002 after a long battle with cancer. John had been a valued member of four of our Practical Mission Teams, and would probably have been on them all if his recurrent health problem had not prevented this, for he had loved Hungary from the moment he first arrived there with us in 1996. Long before that, his wife Elizabeth had rightly acquired the reputation of foster mother to many children in our church, plus those of Christian workers visiting from overseas. In this way Elizabeth, who has had no children of her own, has come to be loved and appreciated by lots of kids as their 'second mum'.

When Elizabeth heard of Mariann's weakness, she immediately offered to go and help. Gillian and I were leaving for Hungary shortly afterwards, so Elizabeth travelled out with us. She had never been to that country before, so spoke nothing of its language. We ourselves knew that Mariann could speak no English, and Lajos's mind is so often moving at such speed that he prefers not to use the quite reasonable grasp of English that he actually has. After a day ot two in Bicske, Gillian and I had to move on to other places, and did so wondering how Elizabeth would cope. Later the next week we swung by Bicske on our way home to pick her up, and then found out.

Elizabeth had been doing really well!

Shy Manasse had taken to her very quickly, and she herself had taken to him, and the twins. Relieved of much of the pressure of work around the home, Mariann had been doing well too, overjoyed with the help she had been receiving with almost everything: cooking, cleaning, washing, ironing and even shopping, all of which Elizabeth had managed without a Hungarian phrase book or dictionary. And Lajos was ecstatic because his dear wife had been able to get some of the rest she needed. "Elizabeth, YOU MUST COME BACK!" he implored her as we left.

So she did, a few weeks later. This time she travelled all the way to Budapest alone, where Lajos gladly met her at Ferihegy Airport. Also, she stayed for longer, and later recalled happily how Manasse had begun to understand some English, even saying a few words of it.

The service Elizabeth had been able to give was truly another of God's gifts to some others of His dedicated people. In its own way her kind of caring ministry is just as valuable as the more commonly applauded gifts of money, training, preaching and teaching, and the rest. And as Chapter 9 will relate, a year or so later He was to honour Elizabeth's faithfulness in a timely but most unexpected way.

****

More recently, yet another different kind of help has been given to Bicske Baptist Church from our own church in Bristol, this time involving two of its leadership team, Mark and Neil. In September 2001 when I was *en route* to Recsk with the Seventh Practical Mission Team, I made a personal detour to Bicske for a couple of hours. This was both to see how things in general were progressing, and to await the arrival of our overland party's minibus from England. Among its load was a new computer system for Bicske Baptist Church. This was a gift from its new sister church in Clevedon, North Somerset, as explained a little later in this chapter.

Lajos had a few items of his own for our private meeting agenda. One concerned another conference in the stimulating series which has been held in his church since it was merely a year or two old. These conferences have become quite a feature of its young life, capitalising on its highly accessible location merely a stone's throw away from the M1 motorway between Budapest and Vienna.

Following the success of earlier conferences for pastors and church leaders, and others on music and worship, as well as the missionary responsibilities of local fellowships, Lajos was beginning to plan one on church planting. The basic question he had for me was this: could I suggest a speaker or speakers who had church planting experience in the UK, and perhaps even elsewhere in Europe too? If I did, could I pass on an invitation for an event whose date Lajos and I would next decide?

Returning home ten days later, I duly spoke with Mark at our church in downtown Bristol. Born of missionary parents in Germany, Mark had been involved in church planting in the Milan and Rome areas of Italy. More recently he has also played a part in establishing a new church in what has been described as 'the largest private housing development in Europe'. Over several years this new town of Bradley Stoke has been taking its amazing shape near the M4/M5 junction. Having gained much experience with Open Air Campaigners too, Mark is adept at the use of a sketch board, and literally has a whole range of conjuring tricks up his sleeve.

Beyond doubt, he would make an interesting and thought provoking contribution to the Bicske conference.

When asked if he would do so, he was immediately positive. "Yes," he affirmed, "I'd be glad to - but would like to bring someone else as well. May I do that?"

The 'other person' turned out to be Neil, a school teacher and seasoned Beach Missioner. At that very time he was preparing to lead a church planting team from our Bristol church, soon to commence its ministry in a sports centre in another of its inner city areas. Certainly together Mark and Neil together would comprise a formidable pair of conference speakers, and have many angles to share on the church planting theme.

So it was arranged, and although I could not travel out with Mark and Neil because of commitments elsewhere in Hungary, I was able to reach Bicske the evening before the conference was due to begin. The programme, involving several other speakers too, was wide and varied. Mark's visual aids attracted particular interest, and Neil made good use of a discussion-prompting questionnaire. The conference was also visited and addressed by both the President and the Mission Secretary of the Hungarian Baptist Union, though delegates came from several denominations.

Although it is not appropriate for us to tell Hungarian speaking people how best to approach evangelism or church planting within the special circumstances found in their countries today, our ideas and suggestions are always welcomed. Across the entire region new ground is being broken with energy and vigour. I have caught some very vivid glimpses of this in situations as diverse as barbecues in the beechwoods of the Mátra Mountains, Christian concerts in city halls with visiting British choirs, basic Bible studies in homes, baptismal services in swimming baths, Gospel presentations in town squares, and 24-hour prayer circles seeking the Lord's blessing on all such happenings.

No wonder God is blessing His Hungarian people... or that, as in the days of the Acts of the Apostles, He is adding to their number those who are being saved.

****

Three months after the church planting conference in Bicske another of our friends from Bristol visited that town for a special purpose. Tim, the gracious Christian architect who has been so much involved in half our Practical Missions, including those in Pápa, Komárom and Recsk had also helped advise on early modifications of the terrapin hut which, as we saw in Chapter 4, has housed Bicske Baptist Church since the year 2000. As a partner in a well-respected West Country firm of architects, Tim is an extremely busy person, but is another who has developed a real 'heart for Hungary'.

While on his way to Recsk with us in June 2001 to help plan the work our Seventh Team were to do there in September, Tim was asked by Pastor Lajos if he could sketch a possible extension to their prefabricated building. That could serve the growing congregation in a variety of different ways. In this regard it should be borne in mind that at least in winter the weather in central Europe is often too extreme for children and young people to engage in any activities outdoors. Tim set down some ideas accordingly, and we then drove on to our other business elsewhere.

The next I heard of the new building plans was during the church planters' conference in February 2002, when Lajos asked if Tim could return in early summer to advise further on that developing project. Spending a long weekend on the job in May, Tim duly measured up the site, plotted the courses of power cables and underground pipes, and helped prepare revised plans to match advances in the new church concept. The finished blueprint allowed for a two-storey building, including a caretaker's flat and several function rooms, in addition to the worship space.

All that remained before the laying of the foundations, hopefully scheduled for September - a tight schedule indeed - was for planning permission to be obtained and initial funds to be raised so that the work could then begin. By the time I visited again in November 2002 the foundations had been lain, though the building had had to be placed further across the plot than originally expected. Lajos explained that the planning officers had called the existing structure a fire hazard, so the new church would have to be separated from it, not linked with it as they had wished. That minor disappointment apart, things had gone very well indeed, though the completion of the foundations represented an unexpectedly tall task.

To find a firm enough base, the sandy topsoil had had to be removed down to a depth of nearly 12 feet, more than twice as far as had been hoped. Still further progress then had to await the coming of better weather in the spring of 2003.

****

A final example of the very special individuals who are increasingly giving expert help to Hungarian Believers in the field involves not one person, but two. Due to a congenital condition, Bob is very hard of hearing, even with two hearing aids. He has long had to lip read, and 'sign' in order to engage in conversations with other people. Therefore he understands the particular problems faced by the deaf of any country, and long ago received a call from the Lord to minister to them in the UK. So for many years he has been a Missioner with the Evangelical Mission to the Deaf, run from a large church in Cardiff where Bob and his wife, Pat are members. Pat supports Bob admirably. For example, although a 'hearing' person, she often 'signs' for her husband.

Bob says that he did not become a Christian until his late teens, and therefore well remembers what life can be like without the Lord. But he also remarks: "The biggest challenge of all that I have had to face was in 1989 when the Lord called Pat and myself to work full-time for Him, reaching out particularly to deaf people like myself. Of course, some of them are handicapped in other ways too. But this has proved to be a real ministry for God for us both. I'm responsible for running three 'deaf clubs', in Cardiff, Bristol and other places where we regularly share news of the Lord Jesus Christ. Salvation is through Him alone! And we have good conversations with some deaf people we visit in their own homes, to encourage them. Often we ourselves are encouraged by their blessings too. Pat's work in a nearby college involves giving help to young ladies with hearing-related learning difficulties. In this secular situation she also has many opportunities to witness both to students and staff. So you see our lives are very busy!"

Gillian and I first met Bob through my sister Brenda, who has long known him well. In 1999 we were trying to find deaf Christians who would be prepared to write their testimonies for us to pass on to Pastor Lajos's wife, Mariann at her request. Before their marriage she was a deaf worker, and has a real heart for the spiritual well-being of deaf people in her homeland. Then giving birth to Manasse and the twin girls in the next three years, she has had little recent time for ministry, but is now picking up the threads again as the children grow older.

With Bob's help I was able, soon after Priscilla and Anna-Abija had been born in the spring of 2001, to deliver to Mariann the five testimonies Bob had collected, including his own. These personal stories had already been translated into Hungarian by our friends Peter and Zsusza in Keynsham.

I shall never forget Mariann's response when I gave her those few sheets of paper.

Scanning them speedily, her eyes brimmed with tears as she exclaimed: "These are WONDERFUL! How can I thank you enough? We will print these as leaflets. This is a GIANT STEP forward for us!"

More recently, Mariann has been further encouraged by the opening of a new international college in Budapest. Run by DOOR (Deaf Opportunity OutReach), its purpose is to train deaf workers from all the countries of central Europe, and parts of Asia as far afield as Mongolia. It also hosts Hungary's very first deaf church, which meets in the college building.

Bob explains that: "It is a special privilege for us to share news of the Lord and His love with many people whom our hearing friends do not fully understand - and now to have the chance to do this in countries other than our own."

For them one such new chance came in 2002, after Mariann had asked if I knew of deaf workers who might be able to visit Hungary to give some guest talks in the DOOR college, and perhaps other places too. I recommended Bob and Pat. Smilingly, Bob mixes his messages and personal ministry with a real sense of fun and excitement about his faith. Pat is quieter, but her warmth and sincerity are clear to all, even those from different cultures and whose sign language is not the same as that used in the United Kingdom.

In October of that year they travelled out at the beginning of an eagerly awaited trip. This proved to be a great success. In a prayer letter on returning home, Bob and Pat wrote about their trip. Here is part of what they wrote:

"We have returned from a most blessed visit to Hungary... the Lord truly encouraged and kept us. We were given very warm hospitality by the Baptist minister, Lajos, his family, and the people of his church.... In Budapest we met the DOOR training centre team: they are American and Hungarian missionaries to deaf people. Each year since 2000 they have run a Bible College. Christian workers come to this from Hungary and surrounding countries such as Serbia, Ukraine, Moldova and Rumania. This year they have a number from Mongolia too! We were greatly helped by Laci, a Hungarian deaf missionary from Rumania who has a burden to plant deaf churches in Hungary, where until recently there was not one. We spent the first morning working out a programme for our stay, and how best to communicate between the American, British and Hungarian sign languages, because there are differences between them all!

"Mariann, Lajos's wife also has this burden, but is limited at present in what she can do, having to care for their three beautiful children.

"One day we were introduced to János, Mission Secretary of the Hungarian Baptist Union.... He wants churches to be more aware of the needs of the deaf. The next day we met with some of them in Budapest, in the first Christian mini-conference for deaf people. Bob and Laci brought the Gospel to those present. Among them were two friends of Mariann's. This was the first time they had been to a Christian meeting. She was so encouraged! Please pray they will seek God.

"On Sunday morning Bob taught the deaf in the new International Church in the DOOR building. There were deaf from Hungary, America, Rumania, Japan - and Bob and Pat from Wales. It was a precious time!

"Another day we travelled with Lajos and Laci to the city of Debrecen in north-east Hungary, near the Rumanian border. It was a four hour journey each way by minibus. We slept like logs that night! But it was worth it. Bob and Laci were able to bring the Gospel to about 45 deaf people in the Deaf Club run by the social services. Pat had prepared a picture Gospel leaflet for the deaf, and the people took all 30 of the copies of it. Laci has requested many more. Bob had a good conversation with one young couple who were very interested. Pleare pray that they will find the Saviour, and that the Lord will save many of their friends and build a deaf church in Debrecen. We will never forget the joy that filled our hearts as we drove back to Bicske that night.

"As we flew back home, my reading from one of Spurgeon's books contained this verse, Isaiah 60:22: 'A little one shall become a thousand, and a small one a strong nation. I the Lord will hasten it in its time.' I was thrilled, for I see this as a promise, both for our work in Wales and in Hungary

too. Please pray that the Lord will fulfil this promise among the deaf in both of these nations...."

In addition to the strong hope from all concerned that Bob and Pat should go back to Hungary again in the future, two other things emerged from their initial visit.

One of these was a translation by Pálma in Bicske of a simplified version that Pat had earlier prepared of J. H. Alexander's book: *From Darkness to Light.* This is the true story of how the Lord saved a lady deafened by childhood illness, and how in turn He used her to bring a profoundly deaf boy to know Christ. This is being printed as a well illustrated booklet for use among the reading deaf in Hungary and its neighbours. Specially prepared for outreach to the deaf, this will be offered to churches all across Hungary, as well as other parts of the pre-Trianon Hungarian speaking region.

Another plan to arise from Bob and Pat's visit in October 2002 was for a residential conference for deaf people, to last a number of days. The Gospel would be presented for non-Christians, and Bible teaching for Believers. The Baptist Union's camp near Lake Balaton would be the ideal site for this, and several invited speakers would lead it - Bob and Pat among them if the dates were appropriate. These were later agreed for May 2003.

On several occasions the Bible tells of hearing people who turn deaf ears to the voice of God.

All too often hearing Christians have also been deaf to the spiritual needs of those who are naturally hard of hearing. It is the responsibility of the stronger members of society to help those who are weaker and therefore naturally disadvantaged. Above all these folk need to be given the message of salvation in ways they can appreciate. In the Hungarian world most deaf people have not actively rejected the Lord. Rather, they have never yet been given the chance to accept Him. How good it is that this is at last beginning to change!

****

In the late 1990s, Gillian and I were glad to help pave the way for a large and focussed group to help in an even more public, and certainly more headline-hitting way in Hungary. This involved fifty members and friends of the celebrated choir from South Wales, *Cambrensis*. Originally drawn entirely from Baptist churches across the Principality, nowadays it has a more varied membership. However, all are Bible-believing Christians and when they sing this shows. Well known for their frequent concerts throughout the UK, and their frequent involvement in radio programmes, including BBC 4's Sunday morning services, *Cambrensis* has undertaken several summer tours abroad, as far afield as Canada and the old USSR.

Through the good offices of Philip and Pearl, choir members I have known for many years from their old Bristol days, a plan began to take shape for *Cambrensis* to have a 'singing holiday' in Hungary in the summer of 1998. This would include two concerts in Győr, and one each in Pápa and Mosonmagyaróvár. For the first time some of the youth section were to join the senior choir, for not all its members were able to make the trip. The teenagers took their chance with enthusiasm and great aplomb.

The trip was timed to fit with the annual Győr Music Festival, a real privilege in that land whose musical reputation in central Europe truly matches that of Wales itself in the British Isles. To secure their official invitation from the organising committee for such a prestigious event, the choir leaders had to submit recorded material for auditioning and approval. After that modest hassle, benefits emerged, for almost all the publicity for the choir's predominantly Christian concerts was then arranged by Győr City Council.

We ourselves also ensured that even the journey out would be a valuable ministry opportunity. For choir members, the very act of travelling by coach to Heathrow Airport and then by plane to Budapest became a special service in its own right. Since the tour fell during the time we had many of the washkits available from the Women's Institutes in Devon to somehow deliver to Hungary, a flash of inspiration and some quick mental arithmetic had led me to a bright idea, and a chance that seemed too good to miss. If, say 40 of the party would agree to take just ten or twelve washkits each in their personal luggage, four or five hundred extra bags would find their way into the country, to be placed at once into the hands of national Christian workers.

And that is just what happened, leading to some interesting moments at the British Airways check-in desk at Heathrow. "Has anyone given you anything to carry in your luggage?" was the standard question put to the vanguard of the *Cambrensis* members as their bags were weighed.

"Yes, some washkits for a charity in Hungary," were the identical replies, time after time.

The check-in clerk was unprepared for the same response from five, then ten and fifteen passengers in quick succession... but then to my amusement varied the usual patter, and began to ask instead: "Has anyone given you anything EXCEPT washkits to carry for them?!"

Praise God that serving Him brings some lighter moments as well as many solemn ones!

Of the more serious yet still pleasurable types, one was specially unexpected. The 'official' nature of the *Cambrensis* itinerary led to a reception for the choir in the Council Chamber in the splendid City Hall - and a short, impromptu, private concert for the Deputy Lord Mayor. As I sat at the back, I wondered if those walls had ever echoed before to Gospel songs such as those being performed spontaneously for the delighted host? Well, just maybe, but surely never before in WELSH!

However, despite such an unforgettable event, the occasion I recall with the greatest pleasure from the *Cambrensis* tour was the two-hour long Sunday evening service in the main auditorium of the old Red Star Cinema, by now well established as the Morning Star Ministry Centre. What a thrill it was to see it packed to capacity with over 300 people, and to hear the choir and congregation worship God together! And the roof was all but raised as, inspired by the choir, its instrumentalists and its excellent conductor we rang out many wonderful old hymns, including that now world famous one originally from eastern Europe, *"How GREAT Thou art!"*

Josef and Wendy, who had done much to facilitate the *Cambrensis* tour from the Hungarian end, including its other concerts in Győr City Hall, Pápa Music School and Mosonmagyaróvár Town Hall, confirmed afterwards what an encouragement and blessing everything had been. It had been such splendid publicity for the Church and the Gospel in the Transdanubian region of Hungary. Press comment described the choir's performance as: *"...of truly international standard,"* and in one single, succinct and well-chosen word, *"MAGICAL!"*

But the press story which delighted us most was of the reporter who, having been assigned by his paper to attend a couple of the concerts, heard the Gospel and came to put his faith in the Lord Jesus Christ as personal Saviour and friend.

****

Last but by no means least in this chapter we should note that it is not just individual people, and groups of people who are becoming involved in helping Christ's heroes out there in Hungary and its neighbours, but also whole churches in the UK. Many have supported our Practical Missions by praying out members of their congregations as Team members, and helping with the costs of the materials and fittings we have had to buy. Many more have helped collect toiletries and children's writing materials to further swell the supplies from WIs in Devon, and some have given or collected toys for Kőszeg's Children's Home, Győr's Mother-and-Baby Unit and elsewhere. But perhaps the most impressive single contributions from a local church 'over here' for a church 'over there' has been a twinning - or, as Hungarians more aptly put it - a 'sister church relationship'.

In September 2000, after our Sixth Practical Mission Team had been glad to help the fledgling Bicske Baptist Church into its newly acquired prefabricated premises, Pastor Lajos had asked Gillian and myself if we knew of any church in the UK that would like to link with them as a sister fellowship.

I remember responding by shaking my head. In all my many visits to churches across the British Isles through 30 years or more not one church leader had ever raised such a question with me. The Lord, though, had plans of His own. Just a few weeks after returning home I had a phone call - totally out of the blue - from the pastor of a church Gillian and I had visited now and again to tell of the Lord's work in central and eastern Europe. For several years this church had had a special link with Bill Kapitaniuk's activities in Ukraine.

"I wonder if you have any suggestions to make," came the unexpected query, "concerning the possibility of our church in Clevedon twinning with one in Hungary. We feel this would enable us to become more fully involved in that area than we can be further afield. Hungary is now reasonably easily reached from here. Our three members who have been with you on Practical Missions are particularly keen to help more, and would ensure that a 'twin' was made to work."

I was astonished, but delighted.

"I think we could help with that," I managed, once I had recovered from my initial shock.

Soon afterwards a meeting was held with leaders of that Fellowship in Clevedon, and we worked through the prerequisites for a twinning that should really benefit both partner churches. I reviewed something of the choice we saw for this in Hungary, and the possible pitfalls to be consciously avoided. Not wanting to set up a possible mismatch, I described several churches we thought might benefit in different ways from a sisterly relationship with that one on the North Somerset coast.

To our considerable surprise, but strongly prompted by the two men present who had been with us to most of the places we described, the Clevedon leaders firmly chose Bicske as the one they would like to visit 'with a view'. I thought how fascinating it would be to see what transpired, for as 'twins' those two churches would certainly not be <u>identical</u>! For one thing there were very obvious differences in language, culture and type of premises. Also, the English church is a long established one with a basically conservative worship style, whereas the Hungarian one has been planted very recently, and has a much more contemporary flavour to its services. This is in keeping with the younger profile of its congregation in that growing town, so close to the motorway and the capital, Budapest. However, if both churches were sure that a sisterly arrangement was of the Lord, then it would surely develop into one that He would bless. From the outset it was even possible to see different ways in which both groups of Believers could benefit.

Merely six months later it was a privilege for Gillian and myself to be with Pastor Lajos and some other leaders from the Bicske church at Budapest Airport to help welcome and introduce a four-man party from Clevedon. This had come to explore the twinning idea more thoroughly before reporting back and, perhaps, making a recommendation to their membership. In the event, they were to be overwhelmed by the love and hospitality of their Hungarian hosts, and specially inspired by the Sunday evening service when no fewer than twelve candidates passed through the waters of baptism in Bicske's borrowed, portable baptismal tank. There was only one recommendation that was possible: the twinning just had to go ahead!

Satan, of course, was not amused. As so often happens when progress is being made for the Kingdom of God, he tried to disturb everybody's joy and peace. One week after the high spot of that baptismal service, the 23-year old son of a Serbian refugee woman who had just been baptised was found hanged. Perhaps this was a suicide, or even murder, for the verdict has been left open until this day. But imagine the impact of that fateful event upon such a young church fellowship!

To make matters worse, at least for Pastor Lajos, a couple of days later his car was broken into and his briefcase stolen. And as if this were not enough, he then went to see the estate agent to whom he had recently made a down payment on a plot of land. On this they would begin building the first house he and his wife would ever have had for themselves and their family. To his horror he found the office empty, with no sign as to where the 'agency' had gone. His painstakingly scrimped deposit had disappeared along with it.

But it has been wonderful since then to witness how, undaunted by those and other unexpected problems, the two churches have grown together in love and practice, praying for one another, and encouraging each other in many different ways. The Clevedon friends were particularly touched the first Christmas of the twinning when Bicske sent every member of the congregation - old or young - a little bag of presents. These included traditional home-made gingerbread biscuits appropriately decorated with icing, a home-made Christmas card, some sweets and a mini notepad. Even the small green, draw-stringed bags enclosing all those items had been specially made for that purpose. They were simple gifts, from people who have little or no disposable income, but who are already setting aside rich stores of that treasure in Heaven of which we spoke of in Chapter 7.

In its turn the Bicske church has also been greatly cheered by gifts from Clevedon. I still vividly remember the late evening I found Kati, Lajos's 'Girl Friday', sitting at the keyboard of the elderly computer in the pastor's office with tears trickling down her cheeks. It was about 11pm which, for early-to-bed and early-to-rise Hungarians is more like well after midnight is to us. I knew Kati had a full time day job too.

"It's the computer," she sobbed in answer to my gentle query. "I have all these things to finish, and the machine keeps crashing. The only way I can get it to reboot is by praying!"

It is so pleasing that, because of the 'twinning', scenes like this no longer happen. In September 2001 the overland party from our Seventh Practical Mission Team were able to ferry out on behalf of the Clevedon church a brand new computer plus peripherals, to off-load at Bicske before the minibus continued on to Recsk, 120 miles or so further east. The old computer which had caused so much woe was summarily consigned to the scrap heap of history, and Kati and others now get to bed MUCH earlier!

****

Finally, a word or two about the future. The Lord is the only one who knows precisely who will respond to the continuing mostly unspoken calls for help from Hungarian Christians in respect of a wide variety of needs, some touched upon in this account and others not. Believers there receive so little help from other quarters that any we can give or organise is welcomed out of all proportion to its cost to us.

Almost any talent, gift or skill that we can imagine could be the answer to some specific prayer - though usually the initiative has to come from us. While Hungarian Christians are certainly happy to accept whatever we can give, by nature most of our friends there are reluctant to volunteer news of their needs. Even with considerable prompting some will still not do that. Thus, the balls are in your court, and mine.

Should you feel that God would have YOU contribute in some fresh way, however strange or unusual it might seem to be, do not hesitate to let **'4H'** know...!

CHAPTER 9

TWO~WAY TRAFFIC

In the half-century prior to the post-communist revolution around 1990, virtually all the Christian traffic with the Hungarian world was from west to east, and there was not even much of this. Since that historic turning point the traffic has been growing - and in both directions, not just one.

So it has been increasingly possible to take and share spiritual encouragement, Gospel challenge, practical aid, resource materials and even modest amounts of money to Hungary and its next door neighbours.

But what if anything has come from that region which has been a help to the Lord's work in our country, and others? In this chapter we will discover some of the new and emerging types of answers to this question.

****

On every one of the seven occasions when Practical Teams have gone to Hungary, members have returned home with memories, blessings and love gifts from the Fellowships we have gone to help. Among my own now quite extensive collection of souvenirs, I cherish most the first that Gillian and I were ever given: a six-inch diameter, reddish brown earthenware plaque from Pápa. We, and other members of the First Practical Team who were similarly decorated, still refer to such items as our 'Pápa Campaign Medals'.

Otherwise we have been regaled with vases, mugs, cruet sets, drinking glasses, beautifully embroidered doilies and many more *objets d'art*. Each and every one of them is a little, yet heartfelt token of thanks from folk whose average wage is still only some £5 or £6 per day. The sentimental value of such gifts is way out of proportion to their cost. Every one has been accompanied by a personalised text or thank-you card… and best of all we know that they all speak of the love and gratitude of those who have given them. How greatly we have come to love our Brothers and Sisters in Christ 'over there'!

Some other tokens of their gratitude have been much more impromptu, though certainly enjoyed by us at least as much. They have included boxfuls of the sweet, pointed, yellow peppers of the kind we have always enjoyed so much at Hungarian breakfast times, and the likes of which we have yet to see in British supermarkets.

Then, for myself, how shall I ever forget the tour I was given of Pastor Imre's greenhouses in Békés? I was taken to see these straight after arriving with Noémi at the end of our hectic, one thousand mile ministry journey in late May and early June 2002 in her parents' elderly and eccentric but also reliable and even loveable Lada car. The cucumber and tomato crops were at their peaks. I was led to two huge cucumbers, growing side by side. Either one was all of two feet long, and as thick as my arm.

"My dad has grown these specially for you" Noémi smiled. "They are the biggest we have had this year!"

I looked at them, rather startled. Quite apart from their size, they would make a substantial dent in my free baggage allowance! Remember, KLM had singularly let me take double the normal weight on my outward journey - but I doubted if they would be too pleased if I tried to make a habit of being over that limit. And I had already accumulated some extra items to replace the flipchart sets I had taken out with me two weeks earlier.

So: "They are FANTASTIC!" I was honestly able to gasp in response to the cucumbers. "But however much do they WEIGH?"

The answer was two and a half kilos each - a total of some eleven pounds altogether. Those two cucumbers would consume about one quarter the free baggage I was officially allowed! But I could not refuse them, and they were enjoyed for weeks afterwards by me, and various visitors to my home.

And then there was the honey. Mike and Kim, who run a smallholding near Taunton, were very energetic members of our

Sixth Practical Team based in Komárom. As we have seen, this stands on the south bank of the River Danube where it forms the present day border with Slovakia. At the other end of the long border bridge stands the now separated Siamese twin town of Komarno.

Hedvige is one of the wonderful working mums in Komárom Baptist Church who give so much to the church. I well recall how Heddi had helped keep our often ravenous gang happily fed and watered. She had also, from the very moment we had stopped trampling on the herbaceous borders around the church building, focussed on them with fork, rake, trowel and watering can and replanted them with a fine array of flowering plants. Although Heddi is married to a Hungarian, István, she herself is a Slovak from the other side of Komarno, where her now elderly parents still keep animals and tend a big vegetable garden. They also maintain a row of obviously very busy beehives.

One evening, thinking Mike and Kim would have much to talk about with her parents, Heddi took them over the bridge for an evening visit. Next morning Mike delightedly showed us what they had been given: several large, one kilo jars of the most fragrant Slovakian honey imaginable, one for each of the men in the Team. It was good we had space in the minibus to transport all those great jars of nectar home. So we and our families appreciated those gifts too, every bit as sweet as they had been unexpected.

However, all would agree that the very best things we have been given to bring back have been the blessings God has showered on us all as we have served Him alongside dear Hungarian Brothers and Sisters in the Faith. Some pertinent remarks about these blessings have ranged from Tracey's meditative: "I've learnt a lot about myself this week," through: "After seeing all the love and devotion Hungarian Christians have for the Lord, my life will never be the same again" to: "I never thought I could be SO BLESSED in such a short period of time!"

And the 'spiritual highs' on which we and our Teams have floated home have been amply shared with others too.

Team members' relatives have often smilingly reported: "He/she hasn't stopped talking about it all since coming back. It has been 'Hungary this' and 'Hungary that' continually!"

Yes, many things, thoughts and experiences have come back with us which we would not have had if we had stayed at home.

****

But then there is another question: "What blessings can friends from Hungary bring when, increasingly, they visit us?" Such visits have so far been relatively few, but will get more frequent in the future. This will be so especially after Hungary's entry to the European Union in 2004. Patterns for these visits, and the benefits that will flow from them, are already being set.

In the middle to late 1990s Christian leaders from Hungary began to come to the UK in ones and twos to help raise awareness of their country, and its needs and opportunities in the 'New Days' it is experiencing now. János, the Mission Secretary of the Hungarian Baptist Union - and contributor of the kind Foreword to this volume - was one of the first who came at that time, with his wife Csilla. Then Kálmán, now President of that growing family of churches came with his wife and daughters. Josef and Wendy, of whom we have spoken several times have come often to underline the sweeping changes that have taken place in official attitudes to Christian activity in their whole region in recent years.

In turn, these dramatic transformation have also affected the responses to us and the Christian faith and message which have been forthcoming from members of the Hungarian general public. For example, our Teams can testify to the growing openness with which passers-by pause and enquire who we are, and what we are doing as we work on the exteriors of churches abutting onto streets, or on the fences or railings which enclose church plots. Such opportunities for them to talk to us, and for us to witness to them, would have been unthinkable before 1990.

Most of those who pause for a chat say how good it is that we have taken the time and trouble to go and help their country in such ways - and how glad they are to be able to converse with us now without fear of personal reprisals.

And, of course, every visiting speaker to the UK from the Hungarian world stresses the urgency of the need to spread as far and as wide, and as quickly as possible, the amazing tidings of the revolutionary love God wants to grant all their compatriots. They stress that they do not take their present freedom for granted. Indeed, many are concerned that several members of the government elected in 2002 held high office as communists prior to 1990....

Yet it is not just what our visitors from Hungary say which impresses their British audiences - but their graciousness and patience too. They display great gratitude for any response to 'the Word' they share, whether expressed in spiritual terms or through some new promise to support them and their kith and kin in one practical way or another.

It must also be stressed that Believers in Hungary itself feel a considerable and growing responsibility for their cousins across their northern, eastern and southern borders, and have been visiting them much more often than they have been coming to see us in the West. By our standards, family and therefore church budgets are much lower in Hungary than in the UK, but those in Slovakia, Ukraine, Rumania and Serbia are lower still. So they show a real concern for their 'next door neighbour' Hungarians, and one which embodies a much stronger fraternal flavour than most normal missionary endeavours. It is commonplace for friends like Noémi and her family to pop over to Rumania to help this relative or that. And church leaders often travel too, like evangelist Árpád from his present home in the western Hungarian city of Szombathely to Rumania for special Gospel campaigns. Increasingly church leaders and workers from Hungary are being invited to participate in camps, conferences and campaigns among all the Hungarian, as well as some of the non-Hungarian, speaking communities in neighbouring nations.

And again, it is worth remembering that such working visits are now taking place not in just one direction but in two. I recall how one of my own visits to Bicske Baptist Church was made all the more interesting and exciting because it coincided with a visit to it by a group of church leaders from Serbia. One of their purposes was to explore ways in which they and their hosts might be able to help each other in the future, particularly in the area of evangelism.

Meanwhile, we saw in Chapter 1 how in recent years many Hungarian Serbs had left their homes in the formerly much larger Yugoslavia and entered Hungary as refugees during the reign of President Milosevic to escape from his recalcitrant regime. This was highly oppressive towards all people groups who were not pure ethnic Serbs. Many of the immigrants were accommodated in a camp in Bicske, very close to the church led by Pastor Lajos. One family that made the move was that of Ruben and Ilona. Fluent in both Hungarian and Serbian, Ruben immediately began to share the Gospel with his compatriots who were billeted in the same place. Much blessing flowed from that, both to individuals and to the youthful Baptist Fellowship.

More recently, now the situation in Serbia has stabilised since the removal of President Milosevic and his henchmen, the stream of Serbian-speaking refugees of non-Serbian ethnic backgrounds has dried up, and the camp is used for arrivals from other countries instead. So Ruben has come to be engaged in evangelistic activities among former Serbian citizens across a wider area of Hungary - as well as back in Vojvodina itself in conjunction with Hungarian speaking churches in that province.

In these and other ways, like other countries of eastern and central Europe Hungary has been until recently a grateful recipient of missionary input, but little by little is becoming also a source of the same. Indeed, it is already a missionary sending nation in its own right, to states as far afield as former Soviet republics in south and central Asia, and even to the still mysterious and remote vastness of Mongolia.

Simultaneously, short-term Hungarian visitors are beginning to help special Christian work in the UK too. Let us catch a glimpse of how and why, through the stories of one group of three, and another of two who came here in the summer of 2002.

****

In late May of that year three visitors from Bicske Baptist Church travelled to England for their first visit to their 'twin' fellowship in Clevedon. One was Pastor Lajos himself, another was his 'Girl Friday' Kati, and the third her Dad, Béla. In addition to the discussions in which they participated on the growing relationship between the two churches, there were opportunities for spiritual ministry from the young church in Hungary to members of the old-established one in England.

Especially memorable was the Friday evening event, when Lajos challenged the young people's group to serve their Lord in a conscious and active way. Afterwards the youth leader was exultant: "In advance I was really nervous about that time, because some of the kids who come are real villains - but Lajos is a natural communicator, and really held their attention, and challenged everyone!"

And for the congregation as a whole, Lajos's Sunday morning message was deemed: "Wonderful!" and: "A fresh breath of the Holy Spirit!"

Though interpreted by Kati, the presentation by the little five-foot-three-inch Pastor was so expressive and so clearly presented that some said: "An interpreter was scarcely needed!"

When the service had ended Mike, one of the men responsible for keeping the sister church relationship arrangement fresh, was beckoned aside by Lajos.

"How many leaders are there in your church?" was his urgent question to a somewhat surprised English Brother.

"Well," Mike replied, quickly regaining his composure, "there is..., and..., and...," as he ticked off the names one after another on his fingers.

"I have a word from the Lord for each of them," Lajos explained. "It won't take long, but could I see the men one by one? I have never done this before, but I strongly feel the Lord wants me to do this."

"It was new to us too," smiled Mike as he recalled this afterwards, "but it was obviously from the Lord. He prayed with us each individually, down on his knees, and shared with us how he thought we should all be developing our personal faith and ministries. I can tell you that off-the-cuff reactions were mixed... but Lajos was spot on with most of His comments, and it is up to us to respond to them in a God honouring way."

Also clearly in the Lord's will was the fact that the visit of the Hungarian trio coincided with the Thanksgiving Service for our friend and thrice Practical Team member John who, as mentioned in Chapter 8 had died of cancer the previous week. It was, of course, his wife Elizabeth who had twice been to Hungary herself to help Lajos and Mariann with their three small children. How appropriate it was that Pastor Lajos was able to a brief tribute to John on behalf of all his friends in Hungary, and to bring words of comfort and thanks to Elizabeth and the family from Mariann and himself.

Two months later, two younger Hungarians arrived in Bristol at the invitation of Neil, who had met them while speaking at the Church Planter's conference in Bicske. Both girls were in their late teens, and relatively new converts: Etelka was about to begin a course at the university in Esztérgom, whilst Ilona was approaching her last year of school. I well remembered them both from my recent visits to Hungary and was glad to see real evidence of spiritual growth in them both.

Why had they been invited to come to England? Mainly to help with a Beach Mission in Pwllheli in North Wales and a Holiday Bible Club in Sheffield, but also to sing and share their testimonies in several churches, including my own. Ilona is a regular member of the small but so-effective singing group in her home church in Hungary, where Etelka helps lead the children's work. A natural extrovert, she has a personal passion for drama, and enjoys engaging in this for the Lord. Over lunch one day in my home near Bristol just before they left on their return journey, I asked what they had found most memorable from their stay in the British Isles. Their answers focused on the thrills of working with a lively Christian group in another country, and particularly of seeing children come to put their faith in Jesus Christ.

Clearly they themselves had been blessed by coming - but in turn they had been sources of great blessings to others too. Commenting on their contribution to those summer outreach programmes, Neil says:

"I would not hesitate to have the girls back... if finances permitted. They had a transparent love for the Lord Jesus, were able to communicate that despite language barriers, and threw themselves into the life of the mission. Both publicly gave their testimonies, sang Hungarian worship songs, and acted in the beach drama. They worked hard in the eleven to thirteen age group, supporting Bible studies and joining in with most of the games.... They also adjusted very well to British culture, and were mature in the way they handled new experiences.... I was particularly struck by the girls' emphasis on intercessory prayer, and their open joy in worshipping the Lord. I trust everything was as much of an enriching experience for them as it was for us."

Other young people from Hungary have begun coming to the UK in increasing numbers in recent years to improve their English. Some of these have also helped in several areas of God's work in this country. One was Anita, cousin of Noémi, who stayed for three months in the summer of 2002. With Gillian in hospital, Anita did much to help keep our house clean and tidy while I was 'visiting', and supported in some of my meetings just as Noémi herself had done earlier in the year. Then there was Zsanett, who worked in Muller's Home for the Elderly in Weston-super-Mare, and Gábor and Tamás in a Christian camp in Norfolk, and... the list is lengthening all the time!

****

So, what can we conclude? For historic and economic reasons this chapter is the shortest in this book. Until recently there was little or no opportunity for evangelical Hungarian Believers to travel outside their country as missionaries, evangelists or, in the spirit of Romans 12, even as short term 'encouragers' or 'helpers'. However, the tide is turning, and the Hungarian speaking churches in central and eastern Europe are fast becoming 'sending' churches. However, they will also continue to be 'receiving' ones for a long time to come.

At present then, what should our response be?

I believe the answer is twofold.

First, we must praise God that the doors into Hungary, Rumania, Serbia, Slovakia and Ukraine are now so much wider open than before - and that our Brothers and Sisters in Christ are so happy for us to help them. Their own vision is so large, and yet their resources are so few. We are glad that they can profit from our knowledge of God's Word, and the techniques and materials we have at our disposal. Any financial aid we can give in these countries where every Pound Sterling goes several times as far as it does here is like proverbial gold dust to them. Above all though, the love we can show Hungarian Christians is a huge boost to these relatively overlooked heroes of the Kingdom of Heaven here on Earth.

Second, we should praise God for the inspirational help which is beginning to reach us in the reverse direction. This is not just through people like pastors and other friends who are coming in person to share with us something of their love of the Lord, but also via devotional aids. These include inspirational new music cassettes and discs from that most musical of all the peoples of the eastern end of our continent. Many of the items are specially written compositions.

There is also considerable potential for Bible games devised by Ágnes in Orgovány, and devotional writings typified by that book on prayer by her husband, Károly to be appreciated by wider audiences.

Most of all though, we stand to gain much from their enthusiasm for the work of the Lord, which is impressive and effective, and greatly infectious too. None of us who visit Hungarian churches ever come home the same as we went, and even when Hungarian Christians come to the UK their shining spiritual qualities make many of ours seem dull and in need of urgent uplift. Their insights into eternal truths have both depth and freshness.

Of course, they are firmly rooted in the Lord, for it was He who brought His dedicated people triumphantly through the fiery trials and persecutions of the past. The difficulties of the 'Old Days' winnowed the wheat from the chaff, giving Hungarian Fellowships of today a strength and purity of leadership which we in the more liberal West can but wistfully admire. Added to this there is the youthful vigour and vision of the younger converts, who are developing their Christian lives day after day with gladness in the liberty their lands now thankfully enjoy.

Perhaps Christian experience across Europe at the beginning of the Twenty-first Century can be usefully envisioned in terms of the 'vehicles' we may choose to ride in as we travel towards Heavenly Jerusalem. Increasingly we from the West are trying to make progress in churches reminiscent of posh, expensive people-carriers while most of our fellow Believers in central and eastern Europe have to jog along in buildings more like battered old-style Ladas, Skodas, Trabants and the like. But, like the teaching in them, these cheaper-to-run alternatives have proved their durability, are not being bought on credit, and are more appreciated for their basic qualities than for ranges of expensive, over-comfortable and unnecessary accessories.

Put more plainly, Hungarian churches may lack many of the 'bells and whistles' which are more and more thought by us to be indispensable - but the faith of their members shines out in a way that puts our spiritual listlessness and lack of warmth towards the Lord very firmly in the shade. The sooner two-way traffic becomes more equal between here and there, the better for us in our apathetic land.

CHAPTER 10

OUR HIGHEST CALLING

Seeking the 'bottom line'

The title apart, it is generally reckoned that the most difficult part of any book to write is the 'bottom line'. Indeed, to pen the conclusion is even more demanding than usual when the subject is an on-going one, as in the present case. Unless the Second Coming of Jesus Christ intervenes, there is much more that Hungarian Christians will seek to do for Him in the foreseeable future - and many more ways in which we could help them.

In trying to select some final principles, and identify some future possibilities, certain themes return to mind from messages I have shared with congregations in recent years. These and other related thoughts came to me first as I sat by Gillian's bedside and thought not only of the past that we had shared so closely, but also the possible shape the future without her might best take. Often it is in times of stress that we listen most intently to the Lord, and wait on Him for guidance for the way ahead. During 2002 I spent more time in prayerful waiting on the Lord than I had probably done in the previous ten years put together. And little did I know during the testing times of 2002 how soon, and how dramatically He would transform my personal situation!

Devotion and distraction

It was Thursday, 24 September 1999. The previous night, Gillian and I had tried to rest as the Boeing 777 winged its lengthy way across eastern Europe and southern Asia to the equatorial island state of Singapore. After all, the days and weeks immediately prior to that intercontinental flight had been as hectic as always before such a journey in preparation for several weeks away from home. But now, following three hours on the ground at Changi Airport, we were airborne again, on the last long leg to Melbourne, capital of Victoria, Australia. It was high time for me to begin thinking seriously about the linking theme of at least some of the 35 messages I was expected to bring in as many days on that particular speaking trip. And I was growing ever more conscious of the fact that the first of those talks was due at a men's breakfast less than 36 hours after our touchdown. Following that they would come along in very quick succession. With such a busy schedule, plus many people to meet in less formal but equally significant situations, there would soon be little time to think!

So, the first question I asked myself was this: "What might Australian church congregations find interesting from the present situation in eastern and central Europe?" Then I wondered: "How could news of that mission field - so close to the UK, but so far from the Antipodes - be made challengingly relevant to many whose lives are so very different from those of, say, the average Hungarian Christian?"

As I doodled with some initial thoughts, two key words suddenly shone into my tired mind. They seemed as brilliant as the rays of the unclouded tropical sun that dazzlingly punched through the rectangular windows of the plane. They were two words which, the more I thought of them, the more perfectly they seemed to describe many of the differences between Hungarian Believers on the one hand and 'Western' Christians on the other - whether living in western Europe, the Americas, Australia and New Zealand or elsewhere. More and more speedily jotting down some relevant sub-headings, I began to develop that double theme which would serve as the basis for a whole range of presentations on our trip 'down under' - plus a number of talks in the UK when we got back home.

And I was to be encouraged on the very first occasion when I sketched these thoughts in public for, at the church door afterwards, one man whispered in my ear: "SPOT ON!" as he warmly shook me by the hand.

So, what are those two key words that had struck a chord with at least one unknown brother? They are DEVOTION... and DISTRACTION.

Even today, as I think of Believers in eastern and central Europe, several particular verses of Scripture spring to mind. One is from 2 Chronicles 17:6, which says that King Jehoshophat's heart was: *"Devoted to the ways of the Lord."* Another, from Nehemiah 5:16 tells us that the famous cup bearer to the king of his day was: *"Devoted to... the work of the Lord."* Meanwhile, in the New Testament, in Acts 2:42 we read that members of the early church were: *"Devoted to... the apostles' teaching, and to the fellowship, and to the breaking of bread and to prayer."* A little later in the New Testament, Paul urges that Christians also be: *"Devoted to one another in brotherly love"* (Romans 12:10).

All this adds up to quite a far ranging picture of devotedness to the Lord, to His business on Earth, and to others of the household of faith.

But what is it that the Bible calls 'devotion'? The Greek and Hebrew words for this in the Bible both carry the sense of 'loving commitment' - and it is to this that we in the West should also aspire as we seek to honour Him, and further His eternal cause. The stark fact is, though, that we seldom reach it... and do so to a much lesser degree than many of our spiritual kinsfolk in lands where persecution has been much more intense, and materialism is much less rife. Many Hungarian Believers are deeply devoted to their Lord whilst, at best, we are often so luke warm!

As I think even now of many Hungarian Christians I know, I recall how keen they are to live for their Lord at work and in the home. I consider too how, even after a long day at work for little pay, their leaders love to serve Him through public ministries, and members of their congregations love to learn more of the Lord and seek Him with undivided attention in worship and through prayer. Not for them some relatively short evening meeting either, for - echoing at least in part the thought of the Psalmist of old - time is spent gladly with the Lord's people and in His house rather than in their own. These are also people who are so glad to respond directly to His Word that the preaching of it is usually immediately followed by a period of open prayer. Then deeper commitments can be made and witnessed by fellowships as a whole. And they are folk who prefer to spend much of their leisure time in the company of other Believers, in communities that not only worship together, but serve and relax together too.

All this adds up to a quality of Christian life that is much rarer in the West... yet which not surprisingly appeals so greatly to unbelievers further east that church families there are generally growing, not contracting as many are in our own land. Small wonder that, more than a decade after the end of communist control, the churches have a confidence that most of ours do not, plus extra degrees of confidence and zest.

Turning to that other keyword, DISTRACTION, what can be said of this, and the people whose experiences it more aptly describes? In the New Testament the adjective 'distracted' is most tellingly used in the Gospel account of Jesus visiting the home of Mary and Martha. Mary was the one who was so eager to glean all she could from the Lord that she gave Him her undivided attention - while Martha busied herself with the housework. In itself this was worthy of her effort, and at least some of what she did seems to have been necessary at that time. However, Luke's point is that by those tasks: *"Martha was distracted"* from enjoying the presence of Jesus. Missing out spiritually, she was the poorer as a result.

Now while Martha is an object lesson to all who know the Lord, her plight is a special warning to those of us who live in advanced market economies like the UK. Having so many things that vie for our attention, to our great loss we are the more easily and the more often distracted from the Lord, His work and even personal consciousness of His presence. It is as if there is some bible of consumerism that urges: *"Having many goods and services available to us, whether we need them or not, we must HAVE and USE them!"* Unfortunately it is also true that the less time we take to focus our minds on heavenly matters, the more earthly minded we inevitably become....

So Martha is a model of many of us in the Western World who know the Lord, and have been called to follow and serve Him, but who suffer the ravages of great distraction, spending much less time conscious of His presence and His power than we should. In reality, of course, things are often even worse than this because in the process resources are often wasted on possessions and experiences we would better do without. Meanwhile, sections of the global

Church that are desperately needy cannot be resourced in ways that might otherwise be possible with our support.

My final observations on this matter are much the same today as they were when, high above the sunlit Timor Sea between Indonesia and northern Australia in September 1999, they first took shape in my tired mind. For one thing, to be able to help God's devoted people in regions like the Hungarian world is simultaneously a blessing and a privilege. For another, as we respond to their more urgent needs our own actually seem to shrink... and with them at least some of the distractions from which we have suffered so much in our materialistic society in recent years.

How much do we owe Him?

Bringing my thinking on these matters still more up to date, I am reminded next of a verse in Luke 16:5 which plainly asks: *"How much do you owe my master?"*

Whenever our Practical Teams are in Hungary we always take time out each day to pray together and seek something from 'The Word'. Sometimes breakfast time has been the best for this, but on other occasions it has been the lunch break or even later. Everything depends on the work programme and how this can most efficiently be organised. Sometimes we have even continued our week's theme in the course of evening meetings with local fellowships, or in Sunday services.

In 2001, for our working trip to the Mátra mountain village of Recsk, I prepared a series of short studies on *Pivotal Questions* that we find in the Bible. From time to time we encounter these in everyday life too - particularly ones like: "Will you marry me?", "Would you like this job?" and, most crucially of all: "Will you repent of your sins and ask Jesus to be your Saviour?" Scripture itself contains many leading questions which, however we answer them, in some way change the courses of our lives.

One of the most life-changing questions Gillian and I were ever asked was popped unexpectedly to us in 1967 in the little sitting room of Bill and Sophie Kapitaniuk's apartment behind the Franco-Polish church they had recently established in Billy-Montigny, northern France. As we saw in Chapter 4, they were SGA missionaries, and we were engaged to be married later in the year.

We were leading a team of young people to help Bill and Sophie - the very first group of this kind I ever led. At that time the Rev. Leslie Edgell was the new General Secretary of British SGA, and was on a fact-finding tour of several European bases of the mission, along with SGA Chairman Frank Farley and committee member, the Rev. Arthur Gove.

To our considerable surprise, one afternoon Gillian and I were summoned to a meeting with the three VIP visitors from the UK.

"We're setting up a network of voluntary Area Representatives across the British Isles," they explained. "We know you are getting married soon, and think that together you would make good reps in south-west England. Would you be prepared to do this?"

This invitation came literally right out of the blue - but we did not have to think or pray long before we said: "YES!"

And that was how our 35 year long commitment to SGA began. As Gillian and I often subsequently said: "We were married to SGA before we were married to each other!" - though, of course, not by very much.

Today Gillian is enjoying her much-deserved rewards in Heaven. Following her Homecall on 30 September 2002 tributes to her flooded in from hundreds of friends all around the world. At her Thanksgiving Service in Totterdown Baptist Church, Bristol on 8 October, special messages of appreciation were presented not only on behalf of the family but also from the local churches where she herself had ministered in ladies' meetings. Still more came from the USA, and from the Christian community in Hungary that she had quickly grown to love so much.

Her brain tumour had been discovered in early February of that year. Details of the poor prognosis we were given at that time were deliberately kept very much within the inner circle of the family until she was taken very ill again in June. And from the very outset of that rocky road I found that new, truly pivotal questions were bombarding my stunned mind. Maybe the most basic one was: "Lord, whatever can I do about our shared ministries?"

You see, in many respects we had been called to serve him together, and had much enjoyed doing so. But this now led to an unexpected problem: believing also in the concept of 'complementary gifting' in married couples, I had had certain well-defined responsibilities in our Christian work, while Gillian had had others. Many tasks, including word processing, emailing, book keeping, maintaining mailing lists, and recording and reporting on our various activities and meetings had fallen into Gillian's realm, not mine. Furthermore, since I had always been well supported by secretaries at work in the University as well as in our office by Gillian at home, by early 2002 I had never even switched a personal computer on! Could I possibly manage everything alone?

Very swiftly, though, I began to receive clear and unambiguous guidance in answer to the more fundamental of my questions concerning the future. Indeed, the whole of 2002 was to become one of listening to the Lord in a much more intent and urgent way than is usual for most of us most of the time. And so I came to prove again and again that old adage that the more any of us listen to God, the more we will HEAR Him speaking to our hearts.

Just two days after Gillian's terminal *Glioblastoma multiforme* was diagnosed on 3 February 2002 she underwent over five hours of palliative intercranial surgery. While she was recovering from it, I found myself reading Psalm 110. The verse that particularly struck me was that prophetic one about the Lord Himself: *"You are a priest for ever."* I knew at once that this was also a word from the Lord specially for me, and that I had to continue with my public ministry, whatever it might take. I had long been conscious too that there is no mention in the Bible of 'retirement'!

Reinforcement of this continuing call to serve the Lord as actively as possible came swiftly through another verse, this time from Paul's second letter to Timothy. The New International Version puts it like this: *"Discharge all the duties of your ministry"* (2 Timothy 4:5). The Revised Standard Version is even more succinct: *"Fulfil your ministry,"* is what it bluntly says.

Could anything be clearer? I think not.

And so I began, with the help of several friends, to learn how our computer works, and to slowly build up confidence in using it. Soon emails were trickling through my fingertips. Documents - including this book - were being laboriously typed into my keyboard with two fingers. And even colour overhead transparencies like those Gillian had so expertly created from my original ideas slipped off the printer for use in deputation meetings, often after many a mistake and veritable heaps of frustration. Such feelings are ones I still experience as I typeset this manuscript, for my thought processes are still so much faster than my typing speed, and my mind often wanders, causing an on-going rash of errors. But David, Shirley (and two of her sons!), Liz and others have taught me a lot, and I am grateful to them all for their gracious help with this. However much I personally: *"Owe the Master,"* I am still not very competent at office work. Thus, I am thrilled that - as I will soon explain - the Lord is now wonderfully promising support for this and other types of practical activities which are all the more vital as *'4H'* ministries to the Hungarian world expand.

We have seen how Noémi, of flipchart fame, was another who became a tremendous, if temporary help to me too, particularly in those sensitive early months after Gillian was taken ill. For one thing it had been a long time since I had taken any responsibility for literature displays in deputation meetings, or for taking money from book sales and tasks like that. The very day Gillian was taken into Bristol's Royal Infirmary for observation and tests a new, temporary but so uplifting pattern for the next few months was set. Noémi came with me to a morning service in Caldicot, South Wales. Decisively picking up the book bags from the car on arrival at the church, she exclaimed: "Leave these to me. I've done this with Gillian a few times, and I know what to do!"

By the time Noémi left for home in mid-May 2002 I had become more used to my new responsibilities. Also, by the time of writing, I can say with gratitude to God that through the whole of those particularly testing twelve months I had to postpone no more than one single meeting, and cancelled none. Some folk suggested that I might want - or even ought - to cancel more, but I was blessed and strengthened in fulfilling that part of my ministry. Through His Word God had instructed me to: 'Fulfil my ministry'. I am thankful to Him for enabling this area of my life to have been so much more normal than much of the rest, and this proved to be a help not only to others but to me too.

In the meantime, spending much time by Gillian's bedside through the summer months of 2002, I also became aware of the Lord's leading in respect of some brand new ideas for resource materials much needed in Hungary - including the Picture Packs and Timelines for Teens - described in Chapter 7. As Gillian slept more and more, so I was able to spend more and more time working on the details of the new concepts, and preparing leader's notes.

Then, at the beginning of August, I suddenly felt constrained to put all them to one side and begin writing a whole new book. This little volume is the result. The all-important first draft was essentially completed just one hour before her body died.... How could I view this project and that timing as anything other than divinely planned? And events since then, especially involving the establishment of *'4H'* have strongly confirmed that they were such, for it was another three months before I had another minute to pick up a pen to write anything else that was remotely imaginative. Without those sad yet quiet hours in the weeks before her Homecall this book would almost certainly never have been written.

In turn those events, and many others that cannot be publicly shared, have all contributed to my thinking concerning the future shape of my own ministry. Above all they have reinforced my certainty that my own primary missionary objective must from now on be the Hungarian region of central and eastern Europe - even if a wholly new Registered Charity is needed to make this possible. There is no doubt in my mind that I must do all I can, in whatever time the Lord will give me, to 'Help His Hungarian Heroes', and do all I can to encourage others to help them too.

At the beginning of this section I recalled the question in Luke 16:5: *"How much do you owe the master?"* For myself I know I owe our Lord and Master all I have, and all I have become. And I know He wants me to continue and extend the work He first gave to Gillian and me to do together here as well as in Hungary and its next door neighbours. Consequently there was one pressing question of my own which I found myself asking Him in return from the very time my dear wife's condition was diagnosed: "Yes, Lord, I know you want me to carry on, and so: *'...discharge all the duties'* of my ministry - but HOW?!"

When I thought of my lack of skills and experience in so many areas in which our work had depended on the talents of my wife, the problems ahead seemed insurmountable. And when I further thought of other significant practicalities both small and large, like how could I possibly travel around Hungary alone with my ten-times-operated-on pair of eyes, my spirit shrank.

In a somewhat different way it was specially scary in late 2002 and early 2003 to contemplate setting up a new, independent charity when for so many years it had been my privilege to be part of a wider, global work. But then I recalled that line of an old Christian song which, accompanied by a catchy tune, goes: *"Though none go with me, yet I will follow..."* and my spirit was strengthened by the Holy Spirit - the One who, according to Acts 5:32 is: *"Given to those who OBEY Him"*.

True, my eyesight may be far from 'twenty-twenty', and things like car navigation can be tricky, especially when the signposts are in Hungarian and the place names are often long and complicated. But His Word promises: *"The Lord will guide you always,"* (Isaiah 58:11) and this promise was enough for me. If I travelled to Hungary in the will of God, He would go with me whether other people did or not. And that proved to be so during my much-blessed trips in May/June and October 2002, and January and March 2003.

Just a little further on in mid-March 2003, as I sit in the Hungarian market town of Pápa, I find I have to substantially revise the original script for this final chapter. And I am thrilled to the core by the recent turn of events that has transformed my personal situation, and given me fresh hope and joy both now and for the future.

Backing up a little, it was on Monday, 27 January 2003 that I called the first meeting of the half-a-dozen friends who had kindly agreed to join me in the *'4H'* venture as the Board of Trustees of this new Charitable Trust. So my long spell of service with SGA has consequently come to an end. This whole experience has been such a privilege, and so richly rewarding! But I must be true to my own personal calling, which is now overwhelmingly to the Hungarian people. Because many of my current ministry opportunities lie outside the present portfolio of SGA's own projects, the time has clearly come to pursue complementary furrows rather than continue in the one that it was a privilege to follow for so long.

In light of all this, imagine my emotions as I recall how, on the very day of that first *'4H'* Trustees Meeting, Rosemary - 150 miles away in Sussex - and I first learned through a mutual friend of each other's existence. Thereby a chain of incredible events was set in motion. Rosemary is a beautiful, warmly sympathetic, resourceful Christian business lady with a real love for the Lord, and a long-standing desire to serve Him in a wider field. After hearing of one another on that day in late January I dashed off a brief note to her, which the mail service kindly delivered all of five days later. Then things moved at breathless speed: Rosemary and I spoke on the phone only five minutes after the arrival of my brief letter - and just five hours later we met at the Reading Service Station on the M4. Such was our rapport that, merely two weeks afterwards I was so certain that the Lord had brought us together in His purposes that I dared ask: "Will you...?" and Rosemary dared whisper: "YES!"

The wedding date was set for 24 May 2003.

What an amazing God we have! Our new 'mission' will be much enhanced by this new marriage. Rosemary and I are certain that our relationship is linked with God's will for *'4H'*, and we look forward with eager anticipation to all He will do for us and others as we serve Him together.

What do we: *"Owe the Master"*?

For all of us who belong to Him the answer is. "EVERYTHING!" Certainly Rosemary and I will be delighted to give Him our new married life, and as many years as He gives us health and strength to serve Him as best as we can.

In the meantime, has this book encouraged you to ask yourself: "What do I owe the Master?"

Perhaps you will feel that at least part of your answer should be somehow related to *Helping HIS Hungarian Heroes*. If so, do let us know. Perhaps that question will, on looking back in the years to come, be seen to have been life-changingly pivotal - indeed not only for you but also for those whom your response will touch for time and eternity.

What is OUR 'highest calling'?

The very last thoughts in this little book initially occurred to me - most appropriately - in Hungary itself. I had been asked to give a talk to the young people's group in Noémi's home church in Békés, the big one described in Chapter 5. Over 40 teens and early twenties were gathered in a large top floor room for my talk one Sunday evening in early June 2002. I had been asked to say something about my scientific work, combined with my personal testimony. As usual on such occasions I wished to end my talk with a challenge.

So, appropriately in a country where almost all Christian workers or pastors also have to earn their living in secular jobs, I explained how for many years my own ministries had been strongly related to my everyday work as a scientist and university teacher. Probably much more than we often think, God is keen that many should serve Him through the special skills and training lay people develop as they earn their living. But I also ventured the thought that in the Western world, as in the Hungarian region and elsewhere too, Believers often settle for some kind or level of Christian service which is lower - perhaps even much lower - than they should.

In Hebrews 8:6 the writer speaks of the 'superior' (NIV) or 'more excellent' (RSV?) ministry of Jesus Christ.

And what was this?

It was His work in sealing the New Covenant with the blood He shed at Calvary. In Békés Baptist Church I suggested there is some superior or higher ministry that each of us can and should do for Him.

Think of any church. Each is like a ministry pyramid, in which every level of service type is significant. But whereas at the base there are tasks like moving chairs and making tea that virtually anyone can do, as the apex is approached increasingly we find ministries which can be properly performed by fewer and fewer members of a fellowship. At the peak itself there is a role filled by one single person - in this case usually the pastor or senior pastor. A mission or charity is similar: there must be many who pray and give to the work, but there can be only one director.

Unfortunately, as I observed to those young people in Békés, there are, alas, too many folk in the world wide Church who settle for personal ministry levels which are lower, maybe much lower, than those of which they are capable. One inevitable result is a generally under-performing company of the people of God.

Why is it so common for us to function at lower levels of service than we should? Lack of confidence in our own ability, or in the power of the Holy Spirit, are often involved. But the biggest single reason is one of personal cost. To serve nearer the limits of our personal ability often calls for more effort, time, money, training or some combination of these than we naturally wish to embrace. How much easier it is to keep our heads down, and leave the more demanding tasks to others!

Take the case of this new Charity, *Helping HIS Hungarian Heroes.* Many have already helped with the precursory work described in this book. But there are many other ways in which help is needed to further the cause of the Gospel in the Hungarian world. The chief requirement for this is resources, of which the human kind is by far the most important.

As I revise this final chapter I reflect on how, just over one year ago, Gillian was apparently in good health here on Earth. Today she is in Heaven, her life's work done. It must also be said that when any saint is promoted to Glory some tasks will go undone unless those who remain behind work harder or more efficiently than before, or new workers step forward or up to adopt more of the strain. I am so encouraged that some have begun to help and support me more since Gillian left my side. And I am so excited and thankful to God that Rosemary and I have been brought together by God for His purposes. That she is relinquishing a full time managerial post in the insurance division of an international bank to join me is something I find both encouraging and very humbling. And our combined prayer is that there will be many others with special gifting from God who will want to serve Him in *'4H'*, even perhaps in more demanding ways than they have previously done in any situation.

Given all the circumstances that have recently confronted me, some people have doubtless said, at least to themselves: "This scarcely seems an appropriate time for a new charity to be brought into the world. Eric has not even given himself time to grieve properly!"

I understand that point of view. Without my overwhelming sense of divine calling in that regard, I would be the first to agree. However as 2 Corinthians 5:14 so clearly puts it: *" Christ's love constrains us,"* and Rosemary and I must be obedient to His decisive leading. And if just a few more were also called to help His wonderful saints in the Hungarian region of central and eastern Europe, there would be still greater cause for rejoicing in both Earth and Heaven.

****

Throughout this book I have tried to describe how, in the Hungarian speaking world, much is different from here. Many Believers give of their time, money and themselves way beyond what comes easily - and yet there are still tasks they cannot attempt, for their numbers and resources are too few. How immensely they appreciate every little assistance given them! And how greatly it encourages them to know that, though often bypassed by the Western world, they are not entirely forgotten by those outside. Yes, they speak a strange language, and from shyness and humility they rarely ask for anything from the rest of the Christian community, but they amply deserve any help that friends like us can give.

So what can we conclude as we approach the proverbial 'bottom line'?

In regard to the quality and quantity of service we owe God and one another, He Himself has set the golden standard. While He was here in this world He served His heavenly Father and us gladly, fully and at the cost of all He had as a man. Where would we be now if Christ had <u>not</u> been obedient to His own 'highest calling'?

Imagine if He had said: *"I love my preaching and teaching ministries... and the miracles I'm able to do. It's so great to give people back their health and strength, to feed hungry folk by the thousands, to make them happy at weddings and even restore life to some who have passed away. But for Me to DIE ON A CROSS, scorned and humiliated by mere men whom I helped create? No, even the very thought* <u>*appals*</u> *Me! I CANNOT POSSIBLY DO THAT!"*

I quoted earlier from the old hymn about obediently following the Lord even if no-one else is prepared to come too. I hoped and prayed that my path to better serve His church in those countries where Hungarian is spoken, and to complement what is being done there by SGA and others in the Name of the Lord would not be an isolated, lonely one. So I am overjoyed that I will be able to make progress for Him with new prayer partners... a new Board of Trustees... and even a new wife by my side!

Rosemary and I have no doubt that thrilling and much blessed times lay ahead as we all serve our great God by: *Helping HIS Hungarian Heroes* .

OTHER SELECTED
BOOKS

Barrett, E. C., *Prime Target, Part of the Story of the SGA.* Slavic Gospel Association, Eastbourne, UK, 1972.

Barrett, E. C. and Barrett, G. M. (eds.), *Glimpses of His Grace: Snapshots of Christian Life and Work in Central and Eastern Europe.* Slavic Gospel Association, Eastbourne, UK, 2001.

Barrett, E. C. and Fisher, D. W., *Scientists Who Believe.* Moody Press, Chicsgo, USA, 1984.

Barrett, E. C., *Scientists Who Find God.* Slavic Gospel Association, Eastbourne, UK, 1996.

Carter, F. W. and Norris, H. T., *The Changing Face of the Balkans.* UCL Press, London, UK, 1996.

Dalziel, S., *The Rise and Fall of the Soviet Empire.* Smithmark, New York, NY, 1993.

Fermor, P. L., *Between the Woods and the Water.* Penguin, London, UK, 1983.

Gardos, H., *Hungary Day by Day.* Pannonia Press, Budapest, Hungary, 1964.

Holmes, L., *Post-communism: an Introduction.* Polity Press, Cambridge,UK, 1997.

Richardson, D. and Hebbert, C., *Hungary, the Rough Guide,* Ehe Rough Guides, London, UK, 2000.

ANSWERS TO CHAPTER 2 QUIZ

1 In clockwise direction from the north, modern Hungary has borders with Slovakia, Ukraine, Rumania, Serbia (Yugoslavia), Croatia, Slovenia and Austria.

2 Hungary has a population of a little over 10 million people.

3 Hungary is largely comprised of the flood plains of the River Danube and some of its major tributaries.

4 The capital of Hungary is Budapest.

5 Hungary's unit of currency is the Forint.

6 Hungary has been a recognised nation state for a little over 1000 years (since 1000 AD).

7 The 1920 Treaty of Trianon was disastrous for Hungary because through it the country lost: (a) more than half its territory; and (b) some one-third of its population prior to that date.

8 1956 was the year of the anti-communist uprising that was crushed by Soviet forces, prompting many Hungarians to escape to the West via Austria; and (b) 1990 was the year when nearly half a century of totalitarian rule finally came to an end, and steps were taken to re-establish a fully democratic system of government.

9 Historically, the Roman Catholic and Lutheran Churches have been the two largest in Hungary according to official membership figures

10 Hungary is now a member of NATO, following many years as a member of the Soviet-led Warsaw Pact.

11 Hungary is due to accede to membership of the European Union in 2004

'4H': A SUMMARY

Helping HIS Hungarian Heroes

OBJECTIVES

"To provide help and support for Bible-believing Hungarian churches and Christians in Hungary itself, and among Hungarian speaking communities in regions of Rumania, Slovakia, Serbia and Ukraine which were parts of Hungary itself prior to the Treaty of Trianon."

ACTIVITIES

Initially, as the Lord directs and enables, *'4H'* will engage in the following types of activities and projects. All represent continuations or extensions of earlier endeavours undertaken by Eric and Gillian, many of which have been described in this book:

1. Organisation of Practical Mission Teams to help renovate and redecorate existing church premises, and convert other buildings for church use.
2. Preparation and production of Christian literature and resource materials particularly for children and teenagers.
3. Presentation of public talks on topics relating Christian faith and belief to aspects of modern life, particularly involving science and technology, either for church congregations or outreach audiences.
4. Provision of aid and other material supplies to individuals or groups within the church or through them to sections of the wider community.
5. Encouragement for churches, pastors, church planters and other church workers through accepting their invitations for preaching, teaching, training and counselling and, where appropriate, in response to perceived personal needs.
6. Support for ministries among the deaf and other groups of disabled and disadvantaged persons.

1. Help to facilitate active links between individuals and churches in the UK and in the Hungarian speaking world.
2. Other specific endeavours as and where possible, requested by Hungarian church leaders and which fall within the general remit of *'4H'*.

PRACTICALITIES

All such activities will be responses to mutually identified needs and opportunities in the Hungarian speaking regions of central and eastern Europe. They will always and only be undertaken after consultation, and in conjunction, with Hungarian church leaders. All will depend on gifts, practical help and prayer support from concerned parties primarily within the UK. Whenever possible *'4H'* will rely on services freely given by others.

In faith, Dr. E. C. Barrett, the Director Trustee of *'4H'*, and his wife Rosemary freely donate their time and services to the Trust, receiving no salary or honoraria for this. The office will initially be in their home and use existing computer and ancillary equipment. The Board of Trustees shall be responsible for oversight and administration of the management of the Charity, as required under UK Charity law.

Gifts made payable to *'4H'* will be welcomed, and will be used without deduction for overhead costs to projects for or within the Hungarian speaking region.

****

Eric and Rosemary Barrett would be glad to add individuals or churches to their Prayer Partners mailing list, and/or to visit Fellowships to share first hand news of the work, and related encouragement and challenge from the Word of God. They are happy to address any kind of meeting, and to do so either separately or together.

Please contact *'4H'* via:
44 Hilldale Road, Backwell, North Somerset, BS48 3JZ
(telephone 01275-463868)